The Light of Many Suns

by the same author

Bomber Pilot
Pilgrimage to the Shroud
The Face of Victory
The Hidden World

LEONARD CHESHIRE

THE LIGHT
OF MANY SUNS

The Meaning of the Bomb

METHUEN LONDON

'Like the light of many suns' was how one observer described the world's first atomic explosion.

My prayer is that the immense forces hidden in seemingly inert matter will ever remind us of the far higher order of power in the spirit of man, the power of love.

'O God, creator of light: at the rising of your sun each morning, let the greatest of all light, your love, rise like the sun within our hearts.'
(Armenian Apostolic Church, Mgr Michael Buckley, *The Treasury of the Holy Spirit*, Hodder and Stoughton)

First published in Great Britain in 1985
by Methuen London Ltd
11 New Fetter Lane, London EC4P 4EE
Copyright © 1985 by Leonard Cheshire

Made and printed in Great Britain

British Library Cataloguing in Publication Data

Cheshire, Leonard
The Light of Many Suns : the meaning of the bomb.
1. Nuclear warfare—Moral and ethical aspects
I. Title
172'.42   U22

ISBN 0–413–59240–5

Contents

Part I
The Last Thirty Days
of World War Two

1. A Summons

In mid-July 1945 an unsuspecting world stood on the threshold of a new technological age. It was one which was to burst upon the human stage so suddenly and with such power that only man's primordial discovery of fire can have remotely equalled it. Small wonder that after a mere forty years into such an age we are still bewildered and fearful, unsure whether the springs of power we have stumbled upon will overwhelm us or be successfully channelled to the common good. Yet I believe that the safe passage of these forty years is of great significance in man's age-long search for the narrow road that leads to those greatest of all human goals, peace and justice among men. I believe that the wilderness through which our zig-zag course since the birth of the bomb has carried us is giving way to the promise of a greener, more friendly land, where the terrifying spectre of world war will cease to have a place, provided only that we measure up to the responsibilities that the ever-accelerating advance of technology imposes.

On the morning of 17 July, the day after the successful test of the first atomic bomb in the Nevada desert, I was in my office at the British Joint Staff Mission in Washington, unaware that anything unusual had happened. My job was to help plan Bomber Command's rôle in the forthcoming invasion of Japan, scheduled for 1 November, and I was applying my mind to a bulky file on the problems the US Marines had encountered in frontal assaults on enemy-occupied islands. It made sombre reading, for the Japanese had amply demonstrated their ability to inflict huge casualties, not only during the seaborne landings, but long after it was clear that all was lost. If this was true on foreign and distant shores, how much more true would it be on their own homeland with three million men under arms and huge stocks of ammunition and equipment? Japan, moreover, lay 450 miles from Okinawa – the nearest American foothold – and Bomber Command would have to operate from 1,000 miles away, or even more. It was a fearsome task that the Allies faced, one which MacArthur estimated would cost three to four million lives and require a full year's fighting.

My mind was preoccupied with other matters, too. The month before I had been taken to meet Walter Lippman of the *Washington Post*, who wanted to put some questions to me about the moral justification of Bomber Command's offensive against Germany. From time to time I had read of the Bishop of Chichester's objections to the bombing of Germany, but his was such a minority view in wartime Britain that I had never given it serious thought, and I was surprised at suddenly being confronted with the issue in Washington. The case that I put rested on the right granted by international law to use such means as were necessary for a successful defence and proportionate to the threat posed by military aggression. After the fall of France and the defeat of the British Army in 1940, with the Navy unable to mount a blockade, and our Atlantic lifeline in grave peril, our one hope was to go over to the attack. Germany's geographical position gave her access to all the raw material she needed; her already vast war production was now boosted by the factories of Czechoslovakia, France and the Low Countries, the majority taken over intact; her army boasted 115 divisions or more, fresh from all-out victory on three fronts, against the battered remains of our 6, and perhaps another 30 being mobilised in the Commonwealth. We faced a desperate situation. It was in Europe that the war would be lost or won, and Europe was rapidly being built into a virtually impregnable fortress, behind whose ramparts systemised terror and oppression ruled. Some immediate way had to be found of carrying the attack straight to the source of Germany's overwhelming and ever-growing military might, and ultimately of prising open a door for the re-entry into Europe. For all its shortcomings, Bomber Command was our only hope, and the trust placed in it was finally justified. Through its severe and sustained disruption of the Nazi war production, and through forcing the diversion of huge quantities of men and materials from the battlefields in an attempt to contain it, the combined RAF and USAF bomber offensives became the equivalent of a second front in their own right. More crucially still, by tying down the greater part of the Luftwaffe and then compelling it to come up and fight, they eased decisively the pressure on the Eastern Front and finally won mastery of the Normandy skies, without which D-Day could never have succeeded.

Lippman conceded that the bomber offensive had been necessary but asked whether its objectives could not have been achieved in a less destructive way. We agreed to meet again to discuss this further, and increasingly I took to pondering the answer I should give. There was an added compulsion to do this because of a most unexpected happening just eight days previously.

My younger brother, Christopher, had recently been repatriated after four years as a POW in Stalag Luft III, and I had taken the opportunity of an Air Ministry planning conference to pay a brief visit to London to see him. The occasion seemed to call for nothing less than a room at the Ritz, and we organised a series of celebration parties. But on the final evening Christopher wanted to spend the evening quietly on his own, and the rest of us went to the Vanity Fair, a wartime bar off Piccadilly. If one was well in with the barman, one could get under-counter whiskey and American cigarettes, and it was a good place for an evening out; but on this occasion the conversation turned surprisingly to religion.

This struck me as hardly appropriate for a last night in London and, with a view to ending it, I said: 'God is an inward conscience, personal to each of us, that tells us what we ought to do and what we ought not; one thing to some of us, another to others. If only people wouldn't confuse the issue by bringing religion into it, the world would be a lot better off.'

'Absolute nonsense,' someone answered with considerable feeling. 'God is a person, and you know it perfectly well. You ought to be ashamed of yourself.'

However unprepared I may have been for the turn the conversation had originally taken, far less prepared was I for its ultimate outcome, for no sooner was the statement made than I knew it to be true. It was not that I had known it subconsciously all along and just needed a jolt to admit it openly; nor that I had followed a process of reasoning which I found unanswerable; but purely and simply that what up until then had seemed nonsense now carried total conviction. It was a conviction that I can equate only with that which comes from direct personal experience, and which leaves no room for questioning or doubt. In the same instant I also knew that from then on there would be limits in my personal life beyond which I could not properly go; perhaps even things required of me that I might not want to do. This made me want to hide what had taken place from the others and keep it to myself as my own personal secret until I was ready to give my response. It all happened in a flash and as far as I am aware the evening just carried on as if the subject of religion had never been raised. But on the flight back the next morning my mind kept coming back to it, trying to weigh up the implications and wondering what the future might have in store.

A week after my return to the office I was ordered to report to Field Marshal Maitland Wilson, head of the British Joint Staff Mission. For someone in my position to be sent for by the Field Marshal without reference to the Air Officer Commanding was most unusual, and the look the two wing commanders who shared the office gave me clearly said: 'You're in big trouble.' The interview lasted less than half an hour. I was told that the Americans had built an atomic bomb, the first of which had been successfully detonated the day before at Alamorgodo. Did I know what an atomic bomb was? No, I hadn't the faintest idea. Neither, I suspected, did the Field Marshal, for he had eyed me intently as he posed the question and relaxed visibly when he saw me shake my head. Having explained as much as either of us was likely to understand, he said that a determined effort was being made to persuade the Japanese to surrender, but if they refused the bomb would be dropped on a target in Japan in the hope of ending the war without the need of the invasion. Britain had played a leading part in the early development of the bomb, and Churchill had agreed with Truman that two British observers would accompany the attack. One was the physicist, William Penney, who had been with the project from the beginning, and the other an operational pilot, myself. I was to learn all I could about the tactical aspects of using such a weapon, reach a conclusion about its future implications for air warfare, and report back to the Prime Minister. General Leslie Groves, chief of the Manhattan Project, as it was code-named, would brief me more fully and arrange for my transport out to the Pacific island of Tinian, where the special duties B29 squadron was based. I was under a strict oath of secrecy and could expect to be shadowed by security.

Carrying such a burden of confidentiality was a responsibility for which I was neither trained nor temperamentally suited, and as soon as I had seen General Groves I left for the anonymity of Los Angeles to mark time until called for the long flight to Tinian, via Hawaii, Johnston Island, Kwajalein and Guam. We were what was called 'processed' through the then principal gateway to the Pacific battle theatre, Hamilton Field near San Francisco, and this in itself was a new experience. One had the impression that the entire United States Air Force – ground crew, administrators and cooks, as well as aircrew of all ranks – was being funnelled westwards through this huge, depersonalised staging post. How long you waited, when and where you could eat, what freedom of movement you were entitled to – virtually none in my case – were all governed by the configuration of holes on a little card they gave you and without which, it was said, you would never leave the base until well after the war was over. No airfield in World War Two can possibly have processed so many personnel so rapidly and relentlessly, with no questions asked, or indeed allowed, and no concessions either to rank or human necessity. It was a frustrating wait, but at least one that gave me an insight into the immense problems the Americans faced in launching an assault force of 5,000,000 men across 6,000 miles of Pacific Ocean onto the beaches of the Japanese homeland.

There must have been more to the little punched card than I had credited it with, for when finally seated at the start of our two-and-a-half-day flight I found myself next to General Farrell, Commander of the Manhattan Project in the Marianas. He was a friendly, sensitive man who, when not working on his files, spoke in terms I could understand about the technical aspects of the mission that lay ahead, the problems facing crews of the 509th Bombardment Group, and the test in New Mexico desert – 'the light of many suns in one; a sunrise such as the world has never seen'. But for the most part I was alone with my thoughts, and these were racing in a way I had never quite experienced before, nor ever expect to again. A new era had suddenly come upon us, a turning point of history, and for some inexplicable reason I had been made a part of its dawning. Admittedly it was only a minor part, but a part none the less, created on the personal orders of the Prime Minister, to whom I would have to render an account of what I had witnessed and what conclusions for the future I had drawn. That in itself was enough to unsettle and throw me off balance, and I began to swing erratically between a feeling of hopeless inadequacy and a misplaced sense of self-importance. The very flight itself seemed to be dragging me away from the known and projecting me towards the unknown. Even the sea we were flying over and the islands through which we staged were different from anything I had seen before. Ahead lay this monster weapon which, through its sheer power of destruction, was about to bring World War Two to an abrupt end. But at what cost, and how had mankind been driven to such an extremity?

Brought up in the aftermath of the Great War, I belonged to a generation which in a hazy kind of way recognised the debt it owed to those who had gone before, but which rejected war as a means of solving differences between nations and believed that war in Europe was a thing of the past. My father, who had served in observation ballons on the Western Front, claimed that I showed not the slightest interest in anything he had to tell me about his own experience of war, and that finally he abandoned the attempt. Why this was so I do not know, for from an early age I used to read books about war in the trenches. These made a profound impact on me. How men were able to endure so much, to face such dangers, to remain so normal and human in the face of all that life in the trenches must have entailed, I could not imagine. Spasmodic though these reflections must have been, they were strong enough to colour my attitudes. There was a day at school when I had caught flu and, clutching my toothbrush and pyjamas, was making my way slowly to the sanatorium, wondering if I could manage the few hundred yards without help. Then the thought suddenly struck me that were I a Tommy in the front line, far from having the prospect of a comfortable bed, I would have to carry on as if nothing were wrong, ankle-deep in mud, and possibly even go over the top with the others. I realised a little shamefacedly that exploits such as these were not for me.

A little later, as was the custom of the day, I had joined what was then called the OTC, where one was given a rudimentary military training. It was all quite fun, undertaken more in the way boys play at soldiers than with any serious intent, but it did give us a sense of identity with the past, and perhaps a first faint awareness of the spirit that moves men and women to place themselves at the service of their country, when the call comes. Every 11 November at eleven in the morning the nation observed the two-minute silence of remembrance. We were too young then to understand its significance, but the ceremony and the solemnity with which it was observed, causing virtually the entire nation to halt its activity and stand silently in a united act of remembrance and thanksgiving, could not fail to impress. It was a profoundly moving occasion which imposed its own authority, transcending everyday values and making one feel part of a greater, almost timeless whole.

One particularly warm and beautiful summer day we had been initiated into the 303 Lee Enfield rifle that had been standard issue on the Western Front, but far from the glamorous experience I had anticipated I had found it decidedly painful, and into the bargain had got very poor marks. On the way back from the range I took a path of my own and for some reason or another sat down under a tree. There must have been something special, even magical, about that moment, for it lives vividly in my memory still today. The spasmodic sound of firing that had accompanied me on my walk had ceased, I could hear faintly the shouted orders to unload, clean rifles, and so on, and then there was silence. It was as if a profound peace had fallen upon the countryside. In a way that I find difficult to describe, everything around me – the parkland, the blue sky, the varied scents of summer, the hum of a passing bee – conjured up an image of all that a young heart hopes for from life, of a future filled with nothing but happiness and promise. Though its significance meant nothing to me at all, it was 1933, the year which saw Hitler's rise to power and the building of Dachau, the first concentration camp.

Five years later, when I was an undergraduate at Oxford, the picture had changed dramatically. War was no longer a distant, abstract threat to be debated and rejected, though debated and strenuously rejected it certainly was; it was now taking concrete shape. The sight of Chamberlain waving his little piece of paper on his return from meeting Hitler at

Munich, looking so evidently pleased with his achievement, edified and gave a sense of relief to some, but not to most of my own immediate circle. Unformed and immature though our judgement was, we felt a disquiet, a feeling of having betrayed a friendly nation, of not having lived up to the honour and the sense of duty that had made Britain the great power she was. I went to my father and asked if I could leave university and join the Air Force, a step which had the added attraction of getting me off my finals. He wouldn't let me, but agreed that I could apply for a permanent commission under the RAF's direct entry scheme, which would take effect immediately after I had obtained my degree. At the medical examination I was asked if I could read the exit sign over the door, made to do knees-up at the double for half a minute, then stretch my hands out to prove that they did not tremble unduly; and, everything apparently being satisfactory, I was passed. The interview board asked nothing much more difficult than, 'What games do you play?', and on being told, rugger and tennis, indicated that I was in.

Had I had the faintest inkling then as to all that was to happen during the intervening seven years, would I have been quite so anxious to join up? How many there are amongst those drawn into the two world wars who must have asked themselves the same question and not been able to find an answer, beyond counting their blessings for having been allowed to survive. Now, as the C54 of Air Transport Command carried us out further and further into the Pacific, the long hours of silent sitting forced me to try and bring cohesion between the peaceful, carefree world of my youth, the shattering experience of war and the unknown that lay immediately ahead. My discussion with Walter Lippman had opened up a new dimension altogether: he had called into question the rights of the bomber offensive, even though he acknowledged it to be essential for the defeat of Hitler. That is an extreme stance; but I was on the way to becoming a Christian now, and this was one of the issues I must be prepared to face and resolve. What might he say if he knew about the atom bomb? There were other questions to be answered, too, even more fundamental than this one, about how we had got into the two wars in the first place, and who was at fault. It was time to look at that, now that I was going to be asked about the implications of the atom bomb for the future of war.

Between the mood of the country upon the declaration of war in 1914 and that in 1939 there was a world of difference, yet also a certain similarity. In 1914 there was euphoria, an air almost of jubilation. A huge crowd assembled before Buckingham Palace and cheered wildly when King George V appeared on the balcony. So large was the throng there on 4 August 1914 that it blocked my father, then a young university don, who was hurrying to Victoria station to intercept my mother, about to leave for a visit to southern France. Astonished by the scenes around him and temporarily halted, he found himself next to an old lady, evidently from a working-class background, who was wringing her hands and saying: 'They don't know what they are doing.' They did not indeed; but neither did their successors.

In 1939 there was no trace of exuberance: just a realisation that the nettle had to be grasped and that war was now the only way out. Somebody put it: 'Time to milk the cows.' Yet a year previously, at the time of Chamberlain's meeting with Hitler at Munich, a large part of the nation had stood aghast at the prospect of fighting. So great was the fear of what Hitler's bombers might do, and so strong the general sense of revulsion against war that, with certain notable exceptions, Westminster and Whitehall were prepared to go to any lengths to buy peace. Most fatally of all, they appear to have been incapable of comprehending Hitler's strategy, and therefore failed to take the steps that could have halted him. Either that, or they did comprehend it but could not bring themselves to face up to its reality.

Reduced to its fundamentals, the reality was clear. Hitler claimed the whole of Europe east of the Rhine as his own personal sphere of influence, and intended to colonise it as Germany's unique Empire. Those elements of the population whom he considered inferior, such as Jews, gypsies, the mentally handicapped, and eventually Poles, were to be systematically exterminated and replaced by Aryan stock. There was never in fact such a stock as 'Aryan', but the term suited his purpose well and sounded better and more acceptable than 'Germanic', which was what he meant. His general aims he had first aired and written about during his days in prison in 1927, and once in power he spoke of them more openly still, indeed even boasted of them. He never disguised the fact that physical violence and terror were one of the instruments he would use to achieve his internal goals, just as his external goals would require military aggression, and he gave the highest priority to building up his armed forces into the most powerful in Europe. Although no timetable had been set, he decreed that the war in the East would have to be fought not later than 1943, when both he and the Armed Forces would be at the peak of their power. But he also knew that military aggression carried its own dangers, and that success would depend upon whether or not he could limit the fighting at each stage to a localised campaign. If ever it should escalate to a full European war, or even if he were forced to fight on two fronts at once, he might well be lost.

Another priority for Hitler was to establish himself in the eyes of his own people as an invincible leader capable of winning against any odds. His occupation of the Rhineland in 1936 and the annexation of Austria a year later could never have succeeded had he been resisted, but he had shrewdly and correctly judged that he would not be. Hitler now needed to eliminate Czechoslovakia as a potential threat to his Southern flank. If he could do that without provoking Britain and France into war, he would be free to turn his entire military might against the East. However he was militarily at a considerable disadvantage. Czechoslovakia disposed of some thirty-five divisions, approximately the same as Germany, and knew that she would be fighting for her life. On the Western and Northern Fronts there were seventy French divisions and a few Belgian and Dutch. Britain had six, but as yet there was no commitment to Europe. Poland on the Eastern Front was an imponderable for which some contingency plans would have to be made. Clearly, one cannot calculate a nation's military power just by counting its divisions, but there can be no denying that, had Hitler's adversaries agreed upon concerted military action, he could never have succeeded. The German high command knew this and warned Hitler that what he was contemplating was militarily impossible, but Hitler replied: 'Don't worry, they won't fight.'

There were, of course, complicating factors which made a problem already fraught with difficulties and danger more complicated still. Britain had world-wide security commitments and was fearful of Japan's expansionist ambitions in South-East Asia; at home she had balance of payment problems, unemployment and a weak economy, as a result of which both political parties had embraced reduction of armaments as a policy. Churchill, who, with a handful of others such as Vansittart of the Foreign Office, did clearly see what was coming, had lost credibility because of past errors of judgement; his warnings fell on deaf ears. Chamberlain and his team of negotiators, it is pointed out, were thoroughly decent Englishmen, brought up to expect at least a degree of honesty and truthfulness in international dealings, and they could not be expected to believe that Hitler was really as evil as the evidence made him out to be.

There was also a widespread fear of bombing and of what would happen to British cities if war were to break out; and this greatly added to the feeling that appeasement was the safest policy. The fact that the Luftwaffe had no bomber with the range to reach England from bases in Germany does not seem to have occurred either to the politicians or to the country as a whole. When war did finally break out, I remember that on hearing the sound of an aircraft I instinctively looked up to make sure it was not an enemy. That was most people's reaction, too.

Those who defend Munich argue that because of these and other factors, Britain was militarily unprepared and France's morale so low after her devastating casualties in World War One that she would not go to war even if Britain did. Consequently, they say, the only option was to sacrifice Czechoslovakia so as to gain time and rearm. But it is questionable that this does justice to France. Daladier, the French Prime Minister, had only reluctantly been talked round to Chamberlain's point of view and had left Munich fearing a hostile reception in Paris. Had Hitler not succeeded in persuading Britain and France to neutralise Czechoslovakia, and thereby place her at his mercy, he would have had either to climb down or declare war. If the former, he would no longer be the all-conquering Führer; there is evidence that some of his generals, expecting this very result, were planning to depose him. If the latter, he would have come out unmistakably in his true colours, and in that event it is hardly conceivable that Britain and France would not have launched their combined seventy divisions against Hitler's western flank. They would have known that their own survival was at stake, not just Czechoslovakia's.

A year later the picture was very different. Germany, who had been rearming five times faster than Britain, had nearly trebled her army to a total of 105 divisions, more than half of them armoured; she had disarmed Czechoslovakia's 35 divisions and taken over all her equipment, including 1,500 front-line aircraft, and her highly efficient armaments industry. Hitler's astonishing success at Munich convinced his generals that they could trust him in all his decisions, that there was no campaign he could not win, no enemy he could not defeat. Whatever their previous stance, the mass of the German people were now wholly won over; he might ask what he wanted and, with the exception of a small but exceedingly brave minority, they would follow him.

By contrast Britain had not made great progress. She still

only had six divisions, and had not yet completed the radar screen round the coast. France had added another twenty divisions, but her morale had dropped further, due in part to the activity of the fifth column; at Munich she had been readier to make a stand than in the summer of 1939. His southern flank secure, and with only three divisions guarding his western front, he was now free to commit an overwhelming force against Poland while Russia attacked simultaneously from the East.

For Hitler, Munich was a moment of supreme triumph, for Britain one of shame and disaster. Yet it was also to prove Hitler's undoing and the making of Britain. Munich had not given Hitler everything he wanted, but it put him, almost unbelievably, within striking distance of his ultimate goal. Had he been content to continue as he had started, with the same caution and astute sense of timing, quietly waiting until French and British vigilance dissipated, as it surely would without further provocation, it is highly probable that he would have succeeded. Prague he could easily have afforded to leave alone now that he had neutralised Czechoslovakia; a sudden swoop on Danzig and there would then remain only Russia who would have had to fight a hopeless single-handed war. But the triumph of Munich proved too much for Hitler and the temptation to march victoriously into Prague too great, with the result that he abandoned the caution that had served him so well and fatally changed what had hitherto been a winning game. First he aggravated rather than allayed Britain's and France's fears by telling them that the agreement had not given him what he wanted and by rearming yet faster still. Then on 12 March he sent his armies into Prague and followed them three days later. Ensconced in Hradschin Castle, the highest point of the city, and looking triumphantly over the lands he had coveted for so long, he thought that his dream of an Eastern Empire that would last a thousand years had virtually been fulfilled. But within a fortnight the picture was to alter completely. On the last day of March, Chamberlain, though subjected to many conflicting pressures, suddenly decided to offer Poland an unconditional guarantee of military support should her territory be invaded. By any standard it was a courageous, indeed a historic, act, one which has not received the credit that it deserves. On Hitler the effect was instantaneous and dramatic. After a few moments of utter disbelief, he banged on the table in a blind fury and shouted out: 'I'll cook them a stew on which they'll choke.'

The unexpectedness of Chamberlain's move threw Hitler onto the defensive, and for the first time he was uncertain what to do. Even with Czechoslovakia out of the way and the military odds overwhelmingly in his favour, he seems to have sensed the danger of open war with the West and decided to try and weaken Britain's resolve to stand by Poland. But this precarious resolve was not to be broken; Britain on her side had also sensed the danger and in her own slow way was clearing the decks for action. On his side Hitler retreated into his eagle's nest at Berchtesgarten to rethink his plans, finally emerging to set about his evil task consumed by an insatiable hatred of whoever might stand in his way. So it came about that for the second time in a quarter of a century an immense multitude of men, women and even children began to leave their homes in response to the demands of a world war, marching forth in the belief, however imperfectly understood, that they were doing their duty and that the future of mankind would to no small extent depend upon their endeavours.

At a personal level my chief memories of those fearsome years are not the moments of battle and danger; in a strange kind of way these have obscured themselves behind a veil of unreality. I can reconjure them if I have to, even make them live for other people; but I cannot remember what it felt like being involved in them; I am not even fully convinced that they really happened. Quite ordinary things can make me nervous, even afraid sometimes; so going into action against guns and fighters has relegated itself to a kind of stained-glass window existence, dramatic and exciting enough, but altogether different from the real world that I know now. My chief memories are of people, perfectly ordinary people who did whatever was expected of them in most extraordinary ways. The ground crews were an example. They spent long hours in a cold dispersal hut waiting for the dawn, or whatever uncomfortable hour it might be, when the aircraft were due back. If their own plane was missing, never to return to its dispersal point again, they used to worry in case there had been engine failure, or some fault somewhere that they had failed to spot. When you jumped down the steps onto the tarmac they always looked so pleased to see you, and once you had gone off for debriefing and eggs and bacon, they got down to removing the cowlings and doing their inspection as if it was their lives, not yours, that depended on it. Never once in four years of flying with Bomber Command did I have an engine failure. It was not only the ground crews, it was everyone, from the lowliest cleaner in the factory where the aircraft were made to the agent dropped behind enemy lines, on her own, never able to relax for fear of giving herself away. The memory that it was the entire nation that fought, and of the way we all held together, will never leave me.

By some strange chance, while marking time in San Francisco, I had happened upon Cyril Falls' book, *The First World War*, in the preface of which I found the following lines:

> I wanted to show what the war meant to my generation, so large a part of which – and so much of the best of it – lost their lives in it. I wanted to commemorate the spirit in which these men served and fought. The modern intellectual is inclined to look with impatience on the ardour with which they went to war. To him it is obsolete. If so, I must be obsolete too. Looking back, the intensity – and dare I add the purity – of that spirit still moves me deeply. I speak particularly of the combatants, including leaders and staff. In the circumstances of that war a large proportion of men in

uniform might almost as well have been company directors, clerks, grocers' assistants or street cleaners at home, for the most part useful, but martial only in appearance and not even always that.

I find in the soldiers other virtues beside courage and self-sacrifice. Though their ardour became blunted, their comradeship never died. Then, though barbarity enters into all wars, they were in general remarkably free from this wickedness that soils the name of patriot.

These words struck an immediate chord within me and moved me not a little, for they graphically echoed the very memories that were just then forcing themselves into the forefront of my mind. How similar, in the terrible task they were each called upon to accomplish, in the qualities they displayed and in their hopes for the future, were these two world-war generations. In the hearts of my contemporaries lay no entrenched hatred, no thirst for battle, no expectation at the end of the day of personal reward. Whatever may appear to those who come after, at the time that one marches forth war holds no glory and very little appeal, except perhaps for a small minority. The cause may do, indeed should do, assuming it to be a good and a necessary one, but not war itself. The closer one approaches battle, the more one wonders whether one will stand the test; the more, too, one treasures all that life has to offer and longs for the untold blessing of peace.

How is it, then, that men and women who desire peace so ardently and who, for the most part, know little of the world beyond the limited confines of their daily lives, come forward in their millions to do whatever may be asked of them and go wherever they may be sent? How, moreover, is it that the great majority find within themselves the power to persevere to the very end through all that world war entails? Were it not for the comradeship and the example of others, for the group instinct for self-preservation, and for the mysterious strength that those with a difficult and dangerous task to accomplish seem to be given, it would certainly not be possible. But there is, I believe, something profounder still. I believe that the inner force which drives man to war against the likes of Hitler is linked to, and derives its strength from, his longing for peace. I believe that each instinctively knows that what is being asked of him, although outwardly destructive, is part of the process of establishing peace among nations. What is sure is that each successive generation is called in its own way to step forward into the unknown and participate, according to the dictates of its own historical context, in the ceaseless quest to establish a better world, one that conforms more truly to the dignity of man. For each generation the call will be different, to some clear and unmistakable, to others obscure and complex, to most fraught with its own difficulties, but to all it is the same voice that calls, the same far-off goal that beckons. Though we may not at the time realise it, we are all involved, all in line of succession with those who have gone before, and all with our own unique and necessary contribution to add.

All the same, I cannot accept that man should ever again be called upon to fight another world war; and as we neared our destination, the small island of Tinian in the Marianas, this thought assumed increasing importance in my mind. We had fought, and been encouraged to do so, in the belief that victory would set us on the sure road to lasting peace. But now that one had time to think about it, could one seriously believe this? What had the propagandists on the First World War meant when they called it the War to end all Wars? And how did their successors suppose that World War Two, once won, would achieve what the first had not? Were they saying that aggressors such as Hitler will never again appear, or that, if they should, those who manage the country's affairs will not repeat the same mistakes? Or had they some new world order in mind? It was yet another unsettling factor, and I felt a great need to identify in spirit with those beside whom I had lived and fought during the past six years. I needed to draw strength from the memory of what they had done and sacrificed, and of why it had all been necessary. That is, I needed the support of the familiar and the known, in order to help me keep my bearings – hold my hand I am tempted to say – as I stepped out onto what was uncharted and unfamiliar territory.

Field Marshal Maitland Wilson's final words as he bid me farewell and Godspeed had been: 'At all costs, Cheshire, see that you get on that plane.' Our last stop-over before Tinian had been Guam, to have breakfast with General Curtis LeMay, Chief of Staff to the Commander in Chief Pacific Strategic Air Force. Six weeks previously I had been told that he might wish to see me to hear about the precision bombing technique that I and one or two others had pioneered in the Dambuster Special Duties Squadron. But he did not seem very pleased to see me when I walked in behind General Farrell, and I had a feeling that something was wrong. I said a short prayer, one of my first since a very young child, that I would not fall too far short of the trust that had been placed in me.

2. Decision to Drop

Tinian was something new in my limited experience. On our drive from the airfield we passed the cemetery in which lay the graves of the 1,100 Marines killed in the bitter fighting to capture just this one small island a year ago. Nowhere were to be seen the extra comforts that we had come to associate with American forces in Europe. The bathroom was just a stand-pipe which emitted either warm or very hot water, according to the height of the sun; ice cream was virtually unobtainable; my billet was a simple tent. This I shared with Bill Penney, the other British representative in the project, an outstanding mathematician who had played a key rôle in the development of the bomb. He looked physically fit and strong, was quietly welcoming, and I immediately felt at home. The night of our arrival there was a main force raid on Japan, and I was invited to Flying Control to watch the take-off. In Bomber Command, where speed of take-off was a highly developed art, we operated a maximum of fifty aircraft to an aerodrome with an average dispatch of one-a-minute. Here I saw 196 huge Super-Fortresses airborne in forty-nine minutes, exactly four-a-minute from four parallel runways. The runway ended at the cliff edge, and the heavily laden B29s, carrying fuel for a 2,500-mile round trip, would lumber painfully off, frequently dropping out of sight below the cliff. That evening one never made it and crashed into the sea. American dedication to the war in the Pacific, and the sheer size and efficiency of their operation, made a deep impression on me.

There were two teams on Tinian: the scientists and the aircrew. The scientists, under the administrative control of Brigadier General Farrell, were charged with the technical aspects of the problem, while the aircrew, commanded by Colonel Tibbetts, were responsible for delivering the bomb. Both teams were amalgamated into one unit and given the title of the 509th Bombardment Group, so that together they were much the same as an RAF Squadron. To the Headquarters unit were added a security detachment and a communications flight, both of which carried their own authority and were not liable to jurisdiction from anyone else, no matter where they might be. The communication flight, with its five C54 transport planes and seven-man crew, plied back and forth between Tinian and Salt Lake City ferrying equipment or personnel as the need arose. These 'Green Hornets', as the aircraft were called, gave the various staging bases along the route plenty of room for thought. Air Transport Command, which controlled all outward and inbound flights, worked to a rigid and stereotyped routine. Every aeroplane that landed, unless it carried the President, the Secretary of State or a five-star general, had to follow the formula, and exceptions were never made. The Green Hornets, however, carried a slip of paper which allowed them to come and go as they pleased and gave them the right to ignore all ATC instructions except those that affected aircraft safety. If they wanted to take off ahead of their turn or refused to take on passengers when their aeroplane was empty, not even a general could stand in their way.

One day towards the end of July a Green Hornet landed at Honolulu on the way to Tinian carrying nothing but a colonel and a major, and a peculiar yellow box which the major insisted on carrying personally. What lay inside it was the nuclear core of the second atomic bomb destined for Tinian, the first having been ferried out on a Cruiser. The colonel and the major climbed out onto the tarmac carrying the box, and for the rest of their stay on the island they never let it out of their sight. The canteen steward asked them to check it in the cloakroom, and when they refused said that it was highly irregular and that he would have to report it. After lunch, while they were preparing for take-off, there appeared a group of senior officers who had been stranded through engine failure and, in accordance with standard procedure, asked to be taken on board. The colonel said he was very sorry about their predicament but firmly told them that he could not help. The general in charge of the party threatened to signal Washington and demanded to know what was in the yellow box, pointing out that whatever it was it couldn't be as important as what he had in his briefcase. To all of this the colonel produced his slip of paper, saying that the box contained his shaving tackle and that if they didn't choose to believe it there was nothing further he could tell them. The incident was not forgotten, and the next time a Green Hornet landed the ground staff maintained a polite but distant manner and saw to it that the crew was processed and off on its way as quickly as possible.

The 509th was more or less secluded from the rest of the island. It had its own administrative and living quarters, and its own operational compound and dispersal area on the north field, all of which were guarded with unusually strict security. If anyone, whether he belonged to the project or not, had attempted to approach one of the aircraft or any of the surrounding equipment without first identifying himself to the guard, he would almost certainly have been shot. One day a small fishing boat came close in-shore immediately opposite the compound. It turned out to be a handful of Japanese fishermen under marine escort who had come to collect more bait. None the less, the reception they were given from the shore batteries made them make for the open sea in no small haste, to the evident astonishment of the marines who knew nothing of the compound.

The compound itself was tucked away in a low-lying stretch of the north shore. It looked across the sound towards the hills of Saipan and opened onto the Navy's anchorage, wherein day and night there plied a seemingly endless stream of ships. It was in this compound, with the three barbed-wired, closely guarded enclosures, that the work of assembling and loading the mechanism for detonating the bomb was carried out. The third enclosure, the inner sanctum as it was called, was the most closely guarded of all and, since only those with 'need to know' were allowed to enter, I felt not a little flattered when they led me inside to meet the physicist in charge, Luis Alvarez, who, I was told, would explain the mechanism for detonating the bomb. What I expected of such a place I do not know, but certainly not what I found. Except for the fact that it was air-conditioned against the humidity and dust, it was just an ordinary Nissen hut, filled with a disorderly array of tools, manuals and instruments of various kinds, and with a perfectly ordinary-looking man bending over a bench. He straightened up and without much formality began explaining the basic functions of the gadgetry around him, little of which I grasped despite his obvious efforts to keep it simple. Then for no particular reason he walked across to a yellow box lying on the floor and casually flicked it open with his foot. Inside I saw what appeared to be a metallic sphere about the size of a football, but since it did not strike me as anything very special compared with the rest of the stuff in the hut I paid little attention to it, until Alvarez said: 'That's the atom.' I must have looked startled, for he told me not to worry; it was perfectly harmless and I was quite free to touch it if I wanted, provided I wore a pair of gloves.

That moment, and the shock it gave me, lives on as vividly in my memory today as does the far more traumatic event a fortnight later over Nagasaki. Disbelief that the new monster bomb we had brought into being could be lying haphazardly on the floor, just one item of equipment among a pile of others, was followed by a sense of awe. Then I pulled myself together, accepted the gloves that Alvarez offered me and touched it. The sensation was rather like that of the first time you touch a live snake: you recoil from what you know will feel slimy and repulsive, and then to your surprise find that it is warmish, almost friendly. The act of doing this prompted an altogether new thought in my mind, unformed and confused at the time, but which has grown in shape and power ever since. Hitherto the bomb had conjured images of devastating, unimaginable power, interwoven with an uncomfortable sensation of having to live with something dangerous and volatile that we could not be sure of controlling. But now I had seen it cut down to size. To look at and feel it was just another metallic object fashioned by the hand of man. True, there was a potentially lethal side to it: but equally an inert side that left it totally subservient to man's will. After all man has come through on his long march through the hallways of time, could it really be that he will not succeed in bringing this new invention under rational and responsible control too?

In the canteen there was a furious Negro driver. He had set out at 11 a.m. to collect the stores, had taken a wrong turn at the crossroads and become mixed up with the convoy collecting coral for the new runway. Having once done this there was no means of getting out, any more than one could retrace one's steps off a crowded escalator. When the convoy stopped at the quarry he was forced to stop too and was promptly loaded up with coral from a steam shovel; when the convoy stopped at the runway, he was forced out of his seat to dump his load. The louder he protested, the more unpopular he became. When he finally regained the canteen at 4 p.m. he was put on a charge for not having carried out his orders. It seemed that the world, too, was caught in a train of events which, having now been set in motion, would permit no escape. That very day, 27 July, President Truman had broadcast from Potsdam the ultimatum that he hoped would persuade the Japanese to surrender without the need for the bomb, and while the Allies awaited the answer there was a momentary lull.

With the fall of Germany in early May it was clear that Japan faced the inevitability of defeat, but the government was in the hands of a military dictatorship, the Gumbutsu, to whom surrender was unthinkable. The losses of the Pacific islands, they argued, were defensive victories because of the huge casualties inflicted on the Americans, and the closer the war came to Japan itself the more the advantage would swing in their favour. Even so the fall of Saipan in the Marianas had forced the resignation of the government and when the aged Admiral Suzuki took over as Prime Minister in April he was given a private mandate by the Emperor to end the war as soon as possible. But he was quickly won over by the military.

There had been a peace faction within broader government circles which had the active support of Togo, the Foreign Minister and the only member of the Cabinet and the all-important inner Cabinet, the Big Six as it was called, who opposed the military clique's fanatical refusal to contemplate the possibility of surrender. The first tentative peace feelers had been made in Sweden as early as September 1944, and now at the instigation of Marquis Kido, the much respected Lord Privy Seal, the Emperor encouraged Togo to initiate an approach to the Soviet Union to act as mediators. An imperial conference was called for 8 June to discuss the state of the war in general and this mediation initiative in particular. The suggestion was rejected out of hand by the military, and instead a resolution that the Supreme Command had prepared was adopted:

> With a faith born of eternal loyalty as our inspiration, we shall, thanks to the advantage of our terrain and the loyalty of our people, prosecute the war to the bitter end in order to uphold our national essence (Kokutai), protect the Imperial land and achieve our goals of conquest.

Because the Emperor remained silent – he was probably too taken aback to do anything else – it was assumed that he approved, and plans for Operation Decision, the final decisive battle on the homeland, were put in hand. Right until the very end, the army would continue to insist that it was here that victory would be wrested from apparent defeat, 'even if it costs a million men'. Later the slogan was to become, 'a hundred million will die', but Japan's national essence will survive.

Everything the military did was done in the name of the Emperor, whose judgement was deemed infallible and to disobey whom was punishable with instant death. The Emperor, however, was nothing more than a manipulative front for the military, who expected him to support whatever policies they embraced. He could lead only by example, for tradition allowed him no political say, and never in Japan's imperial history had an Emperor taken a political initiative. Since the 1930s imperial decisions were obliged to recognise, and accord with, the army's supremacy in all affairs of state. Consequently when at the succeeding imperial conference later in June, the Emperor announced that he would like to see peace – 'not an imperial command, a desire' – the military chiefs were dumbfounded; it was unheard of and unconstitutional that the Emperor should express a political opinion unless asked for and unless it conformed with the Cabinet's policies. Although astounded, they ignored the Emperor's words as soon as they left the palace.

From the very outset of their adventurism into Manchuria, China and then East Asia, the military had presented themselves as the natural leaders and liberators of the region from the alien and effete British and Americans. The speed and comprehensiveness of their early military successes, and their astute propaganda had led the people to look upon the armed forces as all-conquering and invincible. The war had been so remote from Japan that it had made no impact on the ordinary person; only with the fall of Saipan in November 1944, which brought the B29 bomber within range and in consequence forced Togo to resign, did the first glimmer of understanding break through. Even so the military dictatorship duped the people into believing that this was only a necessary price for the victory that would ultimately be won, and when confronted in Cabinet with the inevitability of a direct assault on their shores, they still insisted that final victory would be theirs and that preservation of the national honour demanded nothing less than a fight to the last man.

In the face of this, what were the Americans to do? Admirals Leahy and King thought that victory could be won by air and sea power alone; that is, by stepping up the already devastating bomber offensive and by mounting a total sea blockade. MacArthur thought otherwise, and on 20 April, with the backing of General Arnold, convinced the Chiefs of Staff that he was right, by arguing that bombing was an unproved war-winning instrument, as the battle for Europe demonstrated, and that to occupy a ring of island bases round Japan, as the Admirals wanted to do, would disperse Allied forces even more than they already were, and might commit them to a costly campaign on the Asian mainland. In any case the effect of a blockade would touch the Japanese armed forces only after it had starved the civilian population, beginning with the weakest and most helpless. Although a final decision was postponed to 1 June, plans were immediately put in hand for Operation Olympic, the invasion of the southern island of Kyushu on 1 November, and for Coronet, the assault against the central Tokyo plain, in either March or April 1946. Yet this was a step that no one wanted if it could possibly be avoided.

The battle for Okinawa, the first Japanese island proper to be invaded, offered proof of Japan's staying power and the lengths to which she would go in self-defence. The army lost 120,000 men, forced hundreds of civilians to commit hara-kiri rather than surrender, and made the school children walk across a minefield in front of their army, to spare the soldiers' lives. The battle lasted from 6 April to 21 June and cost the Americans 12,000 dead. If this was how they fought on a relatively unimportant island, what would happen on the mainland itself? MacArthur estimated that the campaign would last a year and cost a minimum of two million Japanese lives and one million American and Allied. In the light of what we now know of the fanatical determination of the ruling military clique in Japan to fight to the bitter end, that was almost certainly an under-estimate. The Japanese Home Army had 2,500,000 men under arms, it was undefeated, had trained 4,000,000 army and navy employees as an auxiliary defence force and enlisted a voluntary militia of 28,000,000 civilians. War production was crumbling, and food very scarce, but the armed forces had 10,000 aircraft, ample stocks of ammunition and equipment and were quite prepared to let civilians starve so long as they had enough for their own needs.

A further worry was that the defeat of Japan would not necessarily mean the surrender of their forces elsewhere. Burma, Malaya, Borneo, Java, Siam, and Indo-China were still occupied, under the command of Field Marshal Terauchi, an aristocrat and fanatical imperialist who totally rejected any idea of a negotiated peace. He had made it very clear that his commanders were to resist to the end in the best Samurai tradition, and had issued written orders for the execution of all POWs the moment the Allied offensive for the recapture of South-East Asia opened. In nearly every camp the prisoners had been forced to dig trenches, at the intersections of which machine-guns had been posted, and under whose enfilade fire they would all die. The start of the Allied offensive was set for 6 September. All POWs in Japan had been summoned and told that they would be shot or killed by flame-throwers as soon as the first American set foot on Japanese soil. In Nagasaki itself they were busy digging tunnels, into which they were to be herded and the entrance then sealed off by high explosive.

In addition it was thought that the Japanese forces in mainland Asia, particularly those in Manchuria, would not surrender without fighting, and ever since 1943 America had been pressing the Soviet Union to abandon its neutrality pact with Japan and enter the war against her. Stalin had confirmed his intention of doing so 'eventually' at Tehran, and at Yalta Roosevelt and Churchill had offered substantial territorial concessions in Asia in return for her participation – the southern half of Sakhalin, the Kurile islands, the lease of Port Arthur as a naval base, a share in the control of the Chinese eastern railway and a presence in South Manchuria. These were concessions which they had no authority to make and were greatly to China's disadvantage.

The alternative was the hope that the use of an atomic bomb, or if necessary two, would administer such a shock as to bring about a change of heart in the military and persuade them to surrender. But this, too, posed problems. When, shortly after taking office in April 1945, Truman was briefed by Secretary of State Stimson about the bomb, the discussion dealt chiefly with the political and diplomatic consequences of using such a weapon, and, in order to consider these and other relevant factors and advise the President, a special 'interim' committee was set up. On 1 June, after much heart-searching this committee unanimously recommended that the bomb be used as soon as possible, against a 'military target surrounded by other buildings'.

> To extract a genuine surrender from the Emperor and his military advisors, they must be administered a tremendous shock which would carry convincing proof of our power to destroy the Empire. Such a shock would save many times the number of lives, both American and Japanese, than it would cost.

There were, however, no scientists on this committee, and many amongst those who had built the bomb had very different views on how the bomb should be used. Stimson asked four leading nuclear physicists, Enrico Fermi, Robert Oppenheimer, Arthur Compton and E.O. Lawrence to investigate these and advise him. With the proviso, 'We didn't know beans about the military situation', they concluded that any attempt to stage a demonstration explosion, as some had been suggesting, was unrealistic. The Japanese would have to be notified of the place and time, and might make special arrangements to shoot the plane down or move their POWs into the target area. Nobody yet knew whether the bomb would explode on the forthcoming ground test, let alone when dropped from the air, and there was the added risk of an unintentional bombing error which might have disastrous consequences. With only two bombs available, and the possibility that the Japs would think it was a stage-managed trick if it were dropped away from Japan in the presence of neutral observers, any attempted 'demonstration' would be unlikely to succeed and might even frustrate the whole project. The only effective way the bomb could be used, they concluded, was against a military target.

Almost all the President's advisors were now agreed that the bomb offered a way of ending the war in the shortest possible time and with the minimum loss of life; Britain had given her assent; and before leaving for the final Allied summit, the Potsdam Conference, Truman had taken the fateful decision to use the bomb. Yet, despite the undisputed probability that it would bring the war to an end, Truman and his advisors still held back. They unanimously agreed that the first thing was to try and persuade Japan to surrender by warning her in the strongest possible way of what would happen if she did not.

The difficulty was how to present such a warning in terms that would satisfy Allied war aims and at the same time make it easier for the Japanese to accept. The Americans were prepared to safeguard the personal position of the Emperor, whom they thought well of and looked upon as an influence for peace. But they were not prepared to do anything that might perpetuate the imperial system, for it was this that had brought the military clique to power, given them their power base and dominance, and which, if not dismantled, could well be used for militaristic ends in the future. This point is crucial to an understanding of the difficulties that the Americans faced in deciding how best to handle the surrender terms, a difficulty compounded by the pressure of war and an inability to understand the military's motives for their suicidal determination to fight to the end.

Roosevelt and Churchill had agreed at Casablanca to insist on unconditional surrender, and, once the military domination had been removed, intended to withdraw and allow Japan to form her own government in accordance with the will of the people. America was well aware of the activities of the peace faction, and through their secret interceptions of Japanese coded transmissions knew before the Potsdam Conference that Foreign Minister Togo, the one effective peace advocate in the inner Cabinet, had instructed Sato, the Japanese ambassador in Moscow, to approach Malik with a view to seeking Soviet mediation for favourable peace terms. Japan had put it to the Russians that they owed their victory over Germany to the fact that she had not entered the war against them, and in this there was a modicum of truth, since had Russia had to defend her Eastern front, the reserve division that tipped the scales when the Nazis were poised to take Moscow in December 1941 would not have been available. Japan also suggested that her fleet joined to the Soviet army would make the Alliance into the most powerful force in the world; but since 80 per cent of Japan's navy was lying at the bottom of the Pacific Russia was not impressed. In any case she was interested only in what would advance her own cause and power in the region, and Sato was just kept waiting in the wings.

America had by now gone through a change of heart about inducing the USSR to join the war. Truman was thoroughly disillusioned by her flagrant breaches of the Yalta agreement and said that negotiating with Stalin was a 'one-way street'. About the atomic bomb he casually told Stalin that America had built a new weapon of 'unusual destructive force'; Stalin showed no special interest and merely replied that he hoped she would put it to good use. Whether he knew that it was an atomic bomb has never been disclosed. With the help of his advisors, Truman now drew up and broadcast the ultimatum to Japan in terms which he hoped would enable the peace faction to prevail over the military, without compromising Allied war aims:

2. The prodigious land, sea and air forces of the United States, the British Empire, and China, many times reinforced by their armies and air fleets from the West, are poised to strike the final blows upon Japan. . .

3. The result of the futile and senseless German resistance to the might of the aroused free peoples of the world stands forth in awful clarity as an example to the people of Japan. The might that now converges on Japan is immeasurably greater than that which, when applied to the resisting Nazis, necessarily laid waste the lands, the industry, and the method of life of the whole German people. The full application of our military power, backed by our resolve, will mean the inevitable and complete destruction of the Japanese homeland. . .

4. We call upon the government of Japan to proclaim now the unconditional surrender of all the Japanese armed forces. . . The alternative for Japan is total and utter destruction.

But the proclamation went on to promise that Japan would not 'be enslaved as a race nor destroyed as a nation', and that the occupying forces would be withdrawn as soon as a new order had been established and convincing proof given that her war-making capabilities had been destroyed.

The proclamation reached Tokyo in the morning of the 27th and produced a mixed reaction. Foreign Minister Togo recognised that, despite the wording of the fourth paragraph, something less than unconditional surrender was being called for and urged the Emperor, the Big Six and finally the full Cabinet that it be treated with 'the utmost circumspection'. Although some were undecided and probably wanted to play for time, Admiral Toyoda insisted that it be rejected and the Cabinet agreed with him. The Emperor and his chief advisor, Marquis Kido, favoured acceptance but did not feel in a strong enough position to say so openly.

A proposal that the official reply be sent through diplomatic channels, and the text of the ultimatum published in full by the press, was vetoed by the military unless a rejection of it was also published. Finally a compromise was reached that an edited version omitting the American concessions be released, but the army forestalled this move by instigating the press to publish an outright condemnation and rejection. Prime Minister Suzuki then summoned a press conference, announced the ultimatum and declared: 'We must kill it with silence [Mokusatsu].' It was an unfortunate term capable in its colloquial sense of varying shades of meaning, but in its literal and formal sense implying a rejection with contempt. The Americans could only conclude, correctly as it turned out, that the militarists were still firmly in control and determined to continue the war to the end. Under these circumstances they saw no alternative but the bomb, and orders were given to prepare for the first atomic attack.

Four possible targets had been chosen: Hiroshima, Kokura, Niigata and Nagasaki, all of them major military complexes, but also heavily populated. Kyoto had been on the original list, but Truman had vetoed it because of its long and important cultural history. The man responsible for selecting the actual target, the date and timing of the attack and all other operational details was General Carl Spaatz, Commander of the Strategic Air Forces in the Pacific, and he was to act in consultation with his Chief of Staff, General Curtis LeMay. The attack itself would be under the command of Colonel Tibbetts, a highly rated pilot with considerable battle experience, chosen because of his outstanding decision-making ability. His primary task was to work out a battle plan that would give him the optimum chance of getting safely through the defences and then ensuring an accurate drop on the aiming point.

This posed considerable problems: the B29 was vulnerable to the Zero, a formidable fighter, and also to ground ack-ack. A fighter escort would not guarantee protection, and in addition would draw attention to the aircraft. Nobody knew the likely effect of the explosion on the attacking aircraft, but it was clear that the fewer there were in the area the better. Tibbetts discovered that by stripping the B29 of most of its armour plate, and all its guns except one in the tail, at his required height of 30,000 feet he would be as fast as the Zero and out of range of ack-ack. Only if the Japanese had enough advance warning of the attack to enable the Zeros to be already positioned above his aproach was there any real danger. It was an inspired decision, but one that startled his crews.

These crews had been carefully chosen on the basis of their battle record either in Europe or the Pacific, and had done an intensive course of training at Wendover in the United States, but they had no inkling of what the mission for which they were preparing would turn out to be. All they knew was that it was something special and that they were not to talk about it. Since their arrival on Tinian on 11 June they had worked in the isolation of their compound and dispersal area, and from there had carried out a number of sorties over Japan with single large-calibre bombs. This had been mainly to test their bombing accuracy from 30,000 feet, but partly to accustom the Japanese to single aircraft, or sometimes formations of three, flying at great heights and dropping single bombs. These flights were not very frequent, and no aircraft were lost. By contrast the other squadrons on the island were operating continuously, bombing from low level and suffering heavy casualties. The 509th was left in no doubt as to what the rest of Tinian thought of them. I went down to the main mess one evening to meet some of the other pilots, but never again; their comments reminded me of the day in May 1940 when I had gone into the bar on Paddington Station to find myself the only RAF man amongst a group of Navy and Army NCOs back from Dunkirk. Even my pilot officer's stripe hadn't saved me from being needled about what kind of cream I put on my hair and whether anyone had told me that an aeroplane was built to fly and not sit on the ground.

I had problems of my own, too. On 1 August Bill Penney had walked into our tent to say that he had a feeling that the Americans were not planning to take us with them, and that in view of our clear orders from Washington something ought to be done. I went off to speak to General Farrell but found him so evasive that I flew to Guam to see Curtis LeMay, Chief of Staff to General Spaatz. He said firmly that there was no room for either of us; in any case he couldn't see why we needed to be there, for we would receive a full written report and could ask for any documentation we wanted. I replied that the 509th thought there was room, and asked on whose authority an order given by Churchill and approved by the President of the United States was being countermanded. He neither moved, nor offered an explanation, nor even smiled. The following morning Spaatz himself came to Tinian to arrange the final details for the attack. Just a year ago he and Doolittle had visited 617 squadron to find out whether it was really true that we were getting what he had called 'beer-barrel accuracy' from high level, and if so, how. He remembered this well and was extremely friendly. But when I raised the matter of the flight he shut right up and left me.

Bill decided that we must insist on an official explanation and asked me to see General Farrell. As always he was friendly and sympathetic, and on this occasion, I thought, embarrassed. He produced a letter which he said had just arrived and which stated that only those whose names were on a list signed personally by President Truman were authorised to go. Since by some unfortunate mistake our names were not on it, he much regretted that at this late stage there was nothing he could do about it, for the President was on his way back from Potsdam, and the attack was scheduled for the day after tomorrow. I looked at the letter and saw that it was dated 20 July, two days after Groves had briefed me in Washington.

Bill and I walked across the camp to get our laundry, which was well overdue, and on the way back had what we thought was a brainwave. Amongst the standing orders we had received on arrival was one that said that all letters, signals or other messages we wished to send would have to be submitted to censorship. That was a fair and necessary ruling, but one that gave us the opportunity we needed. We went straight to the signals office without dumping our clean laundry in the tent first and composed a signal to Field Marshal Wilson which read, 'We are being excluded from the flight on grounds of a technical hitch but in fact this is a policy decision.' The fact that it was going to be censored meant that Washington, and probably LeMay and Spaatz too, would read it on the way to the Field Marshal, and we were pretty certain that something would happen. Most people seemed to think that one bomb would not suffice to to make the Japanese surrender, and that the second would have to be dropped too. But neither of us hoped that this would have to happen. We felt frustrated and rather flat.

Emotionally and mentally it was a tense and perplexing time. On the one hand there were so many technical details to get one's head round; on the other there was the bewildering fact of the bomb. As the hours passed, the pace of life quickened. The work in the compound began earlier in the morning and continued later on into the night, and more and more conferences were called. By the evening of the 2nd the bomb had been assembled and was ready to be loaded into Tibbetts' plane, but there was other work still to be done. The explosion had to be measured and readings of various kinds taken, and there were differences of opinion as to whether the two aircraft that would accompany Tibbetts had all the instrumentation that was needed. The met office, as had been the case with the Normandy landings, assumed greater and greater importance. The Japanese weather seems to be worse even than Europe's, humid with frequent cloud cover. In the month of August there was said to be an average of only seven totally clear days, and the difficulty of making an accurate forecast at so great a range made it almost impossible to know all the seven days sufficiently in advance to make use all of them. A typhoon was in the area on the 3rd, but was expected to have cleared by the 5th. At all costs the bomb had to be dropped in good visibility with a clear sight of the aiming point. Finally zero hour was given as 08.15 hours, 6 August.

Busy though this period was, there were still moments of waiting, and it was then that we put the technical matters aside and pondered on the deeper meaning of what we were about. Each of us on that island had travelled our own individual route to arrive at the final culmination of this ruinous and terrifying war. For some it had been long and fraught with many dangers, for others short and relatively safe; on all it had imposed an inner pressure and tension, and an urgency of purpose that only those who have lived through the experience can fully comprehend. The task that lies before you is not just another task, to be assessed and carried out according to its own merits; it is part of a greater whole which needs to be understood and taken into account before passing judgement on any of its constituent parts. Yet, because of its vastness and complexity, none of us can be sure of seeing the whole in its reality. Whether we wish to justify or to accuse we need to tread warily, and humbly. The active participant will find that he has little time for anything beyond the rôle he has been given.

You are, after all, both the hunted and the hunter. You are aware that there is an enemy ever on your trail, looking for his opportunity to get you. You learn that more often than not it is precisely when you are least expecting it, when things are still, that the danger is greatest. But you dare not let the thought of this ever-present danger enter your mind, for fear it will distract your attention and sap your strength. Mercifully you are given a military training and discipline which turns you from an individual on your own into a member of a team, and which maps out for you the route you must take. It teaches you that you must stand guard over the door of your mind and challenge the thoughts and the impulses that wish to enter, especially fear. Once such a thought has found its way in, you will have great difficulty in throwing it out and so long as it remains you will not be able to operate at your full potential, which your rôle as hunter requires. The enemy is not seeking to destroy just you personally, nor just to overrun and subjugate your country; he is bent on the destruction of the freedom of man to live in peace. What is at stake is the peace of the world, for peace is far more than merely the absence of war. It means harmony and justice, and a society that conforms to the dignity of man. Therefore you have an absolute duty to carry out your task, whatever it may be, to the utmost of your potential.

My own task had been that of a bomber pilot over Germany, but it was not one that I ever wanted. Towards the end of our flying training course, in January 1940, we were asked to state three preferences for our choice of Operational Command. I had read enough of Bomber Command's long and hazardous intruder flights into Germany to know that that was not for me. So I opted in order of priority for Fighter Command, Army Co-op and Fighter Bombers, and was promptly posted to Heavy Bombers. By the time I had completed my conversion course onto Whitleys, popularly known as 'flying coffins' because of the punishment they could take and still keep going, Dunkirk had intervened. With this one's whole perspective changed. The armada of tiny boats that had so astonishingly brought back to safety the 340,000 troops, remnant of a defeated army, also brought to Britain a sense of reality and a different order of priorities. Gone was the time when one could afford the luxury of worrying whether one was posted to one particular Operational Command or another. We knew that a storm of such magnitude was blowing that if we did not quickly pull ourselves together the boat would capsize. Even those who a year previously had been preaching pacifism were now pulling as hard as anyone, most of them; later they would return to the debate, but for the moment very few saw the issue as relevant.

Even so, I have to admit that when on 6 June 1940 I reported for duty to RAF Driffield in Yorkshire I was a nervous 22-year-old man. As I advanced towards the corporal in the guard room I tried to strike the kind of attitude that I thought an officer who had completed his training should, but for all the world I could just as easily have saluted and called him 'Sir' as the other way round. It is common enough experience that when about to face a new and unknown situation we tend to build up a mental picture of what it will be like, only to find how wrong we have been. I imagined I was coming to a land where everyone was a hero and every moment a preparation for battle stations. The formality of identifying myself at the guard room, and the down-to-earth way in which the corporal conducted the affair, took some of the tension away, but I shall never forget the long walk to the officers' mess, wondering what sort of men I would find inside and whether I would make a complete fool of myself. However once inside everything changed. Nobody appeared any different from those I had known at training school; they talked about the same kind of things in the same kind of way, and generally went about their business as if the nightly operations were the most natural thing in the world. The sheer matter-of-factness of it all, the time-absorbing routine to which one was subjected, the realisation that one was a member of a crew whose expectations one shared and must live up to, indeed the whole atmosphere and tradition of the station, calmed and strengthened one's spirit. There was nothing one could conceivably do but keep in step and be carried along by others whom one knew to be stronger and more competent than oneself.

Until September 1943 I remained in Yorkshire, doing three operational tours over Germany broken by a few months as a flying instructor. Then I was told that my bombing days were over, promoted to group captain and given command of RAF Marston Moor, where aircrew underwent a conversion course onto Halifaxes. But I was too young and too inexperienced in admin to be a station commander, and I felt the call to return to the only profession I knew, that of flying bombers in action. Finally they agreed to let me revert back to wing commander, and gave me command of 617, the special duties squadron that had been formed to blow up the Mohne and Eder dams in the Ruhr. Our task from now on was to devise a method of destroying Hitler's most menacing secret weapon of all, the V3. This was a huge cannon, hidden under fifty feet of reinforced concrete which, when ready, would be able to pump a 200lb shell every two or three minutes into London. No known bomb could possibly penetrate that amount of concrete, but Barnes Wallis, who had designed the skipping bomb that bounced over the torpedo nets and destroyed the dams, was working on a revolutionary bomb which from a height of 16,000 feet would penetrate 90 feet into the ground and blow the guns up from underneath. The only condition was that the bombs must land within ten yards of the silo, and from the height Wallis wanted this was theoretically not possible. But the squadron was composed solely of volunteers, all of whom had excelled in one way or another during their previous tours of duty, and between us all we found a way. In forty attacks against selected military targets in France, preparing the technique for the gun silos, we inflicted virtually no civilian casualties. After the relentless sledge-hammer mainforce bomber offensive, it came for all of us as a merciful release.

Bombing is an insidious and possessive occupation that compels your full and single-minded attention. In order to reach peak performance you need to train and retrain day in, day out. You must so master your aircraft that when it comes to action no part of your mind is on the business of flying, all of it on the task in hand. You never see your enemy face to face, but you know that he is stalking you, just as you, in a different sense, are stalking him. Your preoccupation is with the dials in front of you, with striking a balance between the need for accurate flying and that of confusing the defences. You have the needs of your crew to take into account, so as to win their confidence and ensure their full vigilance throughout the whole flight. When you penetrate the target's defences you have to forget evasive action and keep your eyes locked onto the instruments, coaxing the aircraft to stay on the bomb-aiming pointer, as if concentrating on a silver-mercury puzzle. You feel the aircraft lift as the bombs drop, and you wonder if you have achieved your mission, but you give little thought to what is happening on the ground below. You are suddenly much more aware of the defences, and you remember how far you are from home. Around you are other aircraft caught in search-light cones, some of them on fire and falling. Beneath is a red glow; you wish it were larger. Then you return to base. And so it repeats itself time after time.

When you drive past a factory complex you calculate how many tons of bombs it would take to destroy it, and where you would put your low-level markers so as not to damage surrounding property. At intervals you wake up with a start and ask yourself what can have happened to cause you to do this; you know that you have no alternative, but you wish that there was some other way out of the desperate situation into which the world has fallen. The paradox that is man was also revealed in the midst of the relentless slaughter of World War One, by such instances as the British sniper who, when the German in his sights dropped his trousers and squatted down, found that he could not bring himself to pull the trigger.

The question is: what do you do against adversaries such as Hitler and the ruling military élite in Japan? Hitler, as a premeditated and carefully planned policy, set about exterminating whole sections of the peoples he subjugated. In his concentration camps 6,500,000 Jews and 13,000,000 million others were systematically eliminated, the great majority civilians and many of them little children. Every single day of the war an average of 10,000 people died the most terrible deaths in these camps; the closer the end came, the more feverishly the Nazis worked at their extermination programme. Is it to be wondered at that there burned within most of us a feeling of outrage – some speak of it as a deep, steady anger – and that this inner fire drove men to seek the quickest road to victory? Indeed would those who decided Allied policy have lived up to their responsibilities to the human family, had they sought any other road but the shortest?

The enemy we were hunting was not the German, or the Japanese, as an individual, but the perverted system that had taken control of the nation and had duped the greater part of the people into thinking they were fighting a necessary and worthy cause, not a criminal one. Laurens van der Post, who only just managed to survive his long ordeal in captivity in Java and yet emerged still liking and respecting the Japanese, has put this very forcefully in *The Night of the New Moon:*

> I had been made to watch Japanese soldiers having bayonet practice on live prisoners-of-war tied between bamboo posts, and had been taken to witness executions of peoples of all races and nationalities, for obscure reasons like 'showing a spirit of wilfulness', or 'not bowing with sufficient alacrity in the direction of the rising sun'. I saw innumerable ways of killing people, but, most significantly, never by just shooting them. I say 'significantly' because this for me was the most striking evidence of the remote and archaic nature of the forces which had invaded the Japanese spirit, blocking out completely the light of the 20th Century day. It was, indeed, the awareness of this dark invasion which made it impossible for us to have any personal feelings against our captors, because it made us realise how the Japanese were themselves the puppets of immense impersonal forces to such an extent that they truly did not know what they were doing.

I also find this significant because of the fact that the Nazis, in their extermination programme, resorted to ever more tortuous and complicated ways of liquidating their victims. Russians were thrown into concrete mixers, people handed over to doctors for 'medical experiments', most of which had no medical meaning but which finally led to death, millions were transported from one end of Europe to the other, crowded into railway trucks like cattle, when there was no real need. At one stage 70,000 were transferred into three ships, kept in them for six weeks, just out of perversity, and then towed out into Neustadt bay to be torpedoed. Ironically, two were bombed and sunk by the RAF. The Japanese militarists cannot, of course, be equated with the Nazis, for they never even remotely thought of an extermination programme. To them the soldier who surrendered was no longer worthy of his calling and could expect no leniency; they treated their own people in a similar way. But it is yet another proof that Evil is tortuous, incapable of sustaining a straight course. By contrast with Good, which looks outwardly to the well-being of others and is simple and direct, Evil turns inwardly on itself towards its own self-aggrandisement; it is devious and deceitful, and by its very nature ends by defeating its own purposes.

This is in no way to present World War Two as a confrontation between two sides, one wholly good and one wholly bad, for I know there was good and bad on both: much to be admired amongst Germans and Japanese, and much to be regretted amongst us, the Allies. It is that a new awareness of the power of Evil to pervert even the best of us, once it gains control, was forming in my mind. As an introduction to the Christian faith which I now wanted to embrace, I had brought with me C. S. Lewis' *Screwtape Letters* and had been reading it whenever alone. It was a remarkable piece of writing, one which opened up a whole new perspective of our human condition, and left me fully convinced of the reality of Satan as the living, personalised spirit of Evil, the master of deceit, whose objective is the disorientation and downfall of man, and whose existence we ignore at our peril.

Then abruptly the time for reflection was past. The bell had begun to toll for Hiroshima. On the evening of the 4th the seven participating crews were called to the initial briefing, at which Tibbetts told them the full destructive power of the bomb that was to be dropped, but he did not use the word atomic. Admiral Leahy had called it the best- kept secret of the war, and so indeed it was. Even MacArthur was not told until the briefing was actually taking place.

The three selected targets were announced in order of priority as Hiroshima, Kokura and Nagasaki, each having been warned of an impending attack. Three crews were assigned to weather reconnaissance duties, one to each city in advance of the attack; Tibbetts would decide which to bomb only after receiving their reports. One crew was ordered to fly to Iwo Jima as a stand-by in case of emergency. The remaining two crews would accompany Tibbetts carrying observers, monitoring equipment and cameras, but Bill and I would not be with them. As a back-up to the attack, eight other targets were to be attacked by main force aircraft; fighters would be operating at lower level off the coast; along the route would be a series of rescue vessels, in case of need. Finally Chaplain Downey prayed for an early end to the war and a safe return, and the crews were bound to an oath of secrecy. At 02.45 hours on the morning of the 6th Tibbetts' overloaded Enola Gay took off. The previous night Captain 'Peak' Parsons, the ordnance expert responsible for the technical functioning of the bomb, had watched three main force B29s crash on take-off, and he now performed the remarkable feat of arming the bomb after it was safely airborne and out to sea.

3. Surrender with Honour

The advent of the nuclear age saw the simultaneous dawning of another era altogether, that of outright confrontation between East and West. Potsdam, which should have given the Allies common cause in bringing harmony to Europe, instead revealed them as divided and suspicious. In the five months since Yalta many things had changed. The free and democratic elections promised for Europe had been used by the Russians as an opportunity for imposing communism on their occupied countries and subordinating them to control from Moscow. The Americans had not anticipated the Soviet Union's military and political aggression in Central Europe, and now that they saw what was happening were having second thoughts about Soviet entry into the war against Japan. From a military point of view Russian participation offered obvious benefits. It would shorten the war and lead to fewer American casualties, but the invasion would still be necessary, and it was precisely on the beaches that the heaviest casualties would be incurred. For Japan, nothing could be worse than being caught between two invading armies, each of them perceiving the other as wanting to gain as much territory as possible for political purposes. The Soviet demand at Potsdam for a military and political presence in Japan and an equal say in her post-war future finally persuaded the Americans to keep the fact of the atom bomb to themselves, and to go their own way. The Russians, too, were going theirs and hurriedly bringing forward to the second half of August their plans to attack Japan. Stalin informed Truman that Japan had been seeking his mediation to obtain 'acceptable' peace terms, but recommended that nothing be done about it as it was all rather vague. In any case the Americans knew about this, for they had intercepted and decoded the signals, and saw no point in pursuing it, for the reason that they were convinced that the peace party in Tokyo would not prevail over the military. Outwardly Potsdam gave an appearance of unity, with lavish banquets and effusive toasts, but the reality was different. Molotov complained that Truman was too frank with his criticisms, while Truman said: 'You've never seen such pig-headed people.' In many different senses it marked the parting of the ways between East and West.

It was lunch-time on 6 August when Truman, returning from Potsdam on the cruiser Augusta, received the news of Hiroshima. He had spent the morning drafting an announcement, and a renewed and still more urgent plea to Japan to surrender, and this he now broadcast to the world:

> It is an atomic bomb. It is a harnessing of the basic power of the universe. The force from which the sun draws its power has been loosed against those who brought war to the Far East . . . It was to spare the Japanese people from utter destruction that the ultimatum of the 27th was issued from Potsdam. Their leaders promptly rejected that ultimatum. If they do not now accept our terms, they may expect a rain of ruin from the air the like of which has never been seen on this earth.

In Moscow the news brought consternation. Stalin immediately sent for the country's senior nuclear physicists, put Beria in charge of them and told them to produce a bomb at the earliest possible moment regardless of cost. Simultaneously the million or more troops asembled on the Manchurian border were ordered to prepare to attack, and, on the afternoon of the 8th, Molotov summoned Sato, the Japanese ambassador, still anxiously waiting for an answer to his overtures for Soviet mediation. Sato had been vainly urging his government to accept any surrender terms whatsoever provided only that the Emperor retained his throne, and even at this late stage still hoped that Russia would negotiate favourable peace terms. Instead, he was peremptorily handed a written declaration of war.

> The demand of the three powers, the United States, Britain and China, of 27 July for the unconditional surrender of the Japanese armed forces was rejected by Japan. Thus the proposal made by the Japanese government to the Soviet Union for mediation in the Far East has lost all foundation.
>
> Taking into account the refusal of Japan to capitulate, the Allies approached the Soviet government with a proposal to join the war against Japanese aggression and thus shorten the duration of the war, reduce the number of casualties and contribute towards the most speedy restoration of peace.
>
> True to its obligation as an Ally, the Soviet government accepted the proposal of the Allies and has joined in the declaration of the Allied powers of 27 July.
>
> The Soviet government considers that this policy is the only means able to bring peace nearer, to free the people from further sacrifice and suffering and to give the Japanese people the opportunity of avoiding the danger of destruction suffered by Germany after her refusal to accept unconditional surrender.
>
> In view of the above, the Soviet government declares that from tomorrow, that is from 9 August, the Soviet Union will consider herself in a state of war against Japan.

That very same day the Soviet army invaded Manchuria, to add huge territorial gains to those already promised at Yalta. Of the 250,000 prisoners-of-war whom they took in their rapid advance against the already weakened Kwangtung Army, only half ever returned home, and these years later. Yet the war was over in a week.

The impact that Hiroshima made on Tokyo was far less than on the rest of the world. To Foreign Minister Togo and the peace party it seemed the hoped-for way of capitulating without laying the blame at the army's door. If the bomb was what Truman claimed, a new weapon of unheard-of destructive force, then fighting against it was impossible. The others, however, saw it differently. Japan had a small atomic research programme of its own, but few in the government knew of this, the majority had not the slightest idea what 'atomic' meant and many took Truman's dramatic announcement as just a propaganda ploy. Military circles argued that the USA did not have the capability to transport what was obviously a highly unstable mechanism across the whole Pacific and then deliver it accurately on a target. To have done it once, even if true, was no proof that they could do it again. The news that a whole city had been destroyed was disturbing, indeed, and another proof of the military's inability to protect the homeland. But in a city that had already been devasted by bombs and incendiaries, and was being attacked almost continuously, this was not something altogether new.

The fall of Saipan, 1,250 miles to the south, had brought Japan well within range of the revolutionary and powerful B29 bomber that was ready for service in October 1944. The initial attacks, aimed at destroying Japanese war production, had been carried out from 27,000 feet and above, and had proved neither accurate nor effective. Apart from inadequate bombing techniques, the targets were all too often obscured by the winter cloud. But Curtis LeMay, who arrived to take command of the Marianas in spring, decided on a new policy of low-level bombing by night, a tactic made possible by the relatively weak Japanese night-time defences. This new offensive opened on 9 March with an incendiary attack on Tokyo that killed 83,793 people and rendered 1,000,000 homeless. From then onwards, though sustaining heavy casualties themselves, American bombers ranged the length and breadth of Japan in the hope of finishing the war without the need for an invasion. That the Japanese people managed to survive this onslaught is remarkable indeed. In just five months they suffered a devastation comparable with that inflicted on Germany by five years of Allied bombing: 300,000 civilians were killed, 430,000 injured and more than

9,000,000 made homeless. War production was virtually brought to a halt, whole cities destroyed and, as a result of the Navy's blockade, food was running short. Given this, it was perhaps not surprising that the Japanese military mind, which in any case looked upon civilians as second-class and expendable citizens, did not regard the instant destruction of Hiroshima as a reason for laying down their arms. In reply to Togo's insistence that the whole course and shape of the war had been changed by the atomic bomb, the War Minister, General Anami, restated the military view that the outcome of the war depended not on bombs but on the final and decisive battle on the homeland's beaches.

The American conviction that only an extreme measure would persuade Japan to surrender was not a mistaken one. In the space of forty-eight hours the military had suffered two shattering blows – the bomb and the Soviet invasion of Manchuria – without their resolve to hold on to the very end being dented. Of these two it was the latter that made the greater immediate impact, for, as it fell within the realm of their experience, its consequences were easy enough to calculate. The bomb, on the other hand, was something entirely new. As is usually the case when we come face to face with the unknown, it created amongst the military an unease, but for the moment it could be dismissed until there was more evidence as to what the American claim implied.

The Americans had always thought that two bombs would be needed; the first to convince Japan that they had an atomic bomb, and the second to demonstrate their capability and will to continue dropping them until she surrendered. Once it was clear that the military had overruled the peace faction, the second attack had to come quickly in order to leave the Japanese in no possible doubt that Truman meant what he had said. The weather was closing in over Japan and the met office had estimated that the only foreseeable clear day in the next fortnight was the 9th. This left no latitude for postponement, and the decision to launch the second bomb was taken.

At about the same hour that Molotov was seeing Sato, Bill and I received the signal clearing us as observers on the second atomic raid. It was only just in time, for briefing was due six hours later at 20.00 hours. Instructions required that we sleep in the afternoon, but the weather was very hot and the tents cut out neither the heat nor the light, so we were issued with sleeping pills. The Hiroshima crews had found that these did not work, and at briefing they had been given Benzedrine to wake them up. I refused my sleeping pills, for I preferred to be tired than drugged. Briefing was almost the same as the one three nights previously, except that this time everybody knew that the bomb we would be carrying was an atomic one. The only difference between the two bombs was that the first had been uranium, and this one plutonium, the same as tested in the New Mexican desert. It was ten feet eight inches long and five feet in diameter, and nicknamed 'Fat man'. Because of the many electronic and other complicated circuits that were needed to keep it in a state of readiness, a black box was fitted to the aircraft which monitored how these circuits were functioning. Commander Frederick Ashworth, a leading figure in the development of the bomb, was the only man on the island who fully understood the box, and his eyes hardly left it for the whole time of the outward flight. To help him, he had an electronics counter-measure expert, Jake Beser, for there was always the possibility that the Japanese might succeed in detonating the bomb while it was still in the aircraft. As at Hiroshima, it was set to explode at 2,000 feet, in order to cause maximum blast effect and to minimise radiation, but this required a complicated detonation mechanism and there was no guarantee that it would work. It could not be armed once loaded into the bomb bay, and was live on take-off.

For this attack only two targets were given, Kokura and Nagasaki, in that order of priority; as before, leaflets warning of an attack had already been dropped on each of them. The crews that were to report weather conditions over the two cities in advance of the strike plane's arrival were chosen with special care because of the importance of not making a mistake. Once airborne, the bomb could not be brought back. The strike plane was under the command of Major Charles Sweeney, who had piloted the instrument carrying aircraft that accompanied Tibbetts over Hiroshima. As this was still fitted out with its special instruments, Sweeney changed planes with Captain Bock. Sweeney carried the bomb in the 'Bock's Car', while Bock in the 'Great Artiste' carried the instrument capsule that was to be dropped one mile behind the bomb. Taped to this capsule was a message from Alvarez and two of the other scientists on Tinian to the Japanese nuclear physicist, Professor Sagani, pleading with him to seek peace. Sagani had worked with the three of them before the war at the University of California, and he would know only too well what an atom bomb meant. Amongst the scientific team in Bock's plane was William L. Laurence of the *New York Times,* whose series of articles on the bomb was later to earn him a Pulitzer prize. The third plane, carrying a high-speed camera and other instruments and observers, including Bill and myself, was flown by Major Jim Hopkins.

Once again Chaplain Downey prayed for the safety of the crews and an early return of peace. He read the prayer with great depth of feeling and, though I cannot say why, for I believed that what we were about to do would end the war, and I had come to believe too, that prayer is necessary, I was taken a little by surprise. We then went to the mess for the customary midnight breakfast, wished each other well and went to our individual aircraft. Sweeney arrived at his, 'Bock's Car', to find his flight engineer a worried man. The pre-flight check-up had revealed that the fuel transfer pump on the bomb bay auxiliary tank was inoperative, which meant that none of the 600 gallons it contained could be used. Tibbetts left the decision to Sweeney, and Sweeney said that he would go. There was little else he could do.

At 02.00 hours I climbed into the Hopkins' aircraft and made myself as comfortable as possible in a bucket seat next to Bill. It was his first operational sortie, and I rather hoped there would be signs of nervousness, but there were none. The target was seven hours flying time away, and once we were safely airborne I rolled up on the floor and went to sleep. The three aircraft should have been flying in loose formation, but there was bad weather ahead, in the form of a line squall just short of Iwo Jima, so we flew independently with orders to rendezvous at 07.00 over the island of Yaku Shima, south of Kyushu. The turbulence of the squall caused Hopkins to climb up to 39,000 feet, and on arrival at Yaku Shima he stayed at that height, 9,000 feet higher than he should have been, and started doing 50-mile dog legs instead of orbiting as ordered. It struck me as an extraordinary thing to do, and I would have queried it but for the fact that he had just invited me forward into the cockpit. I was the only one there other than the crew and felt too privileged to do anything other than thank him. At 07.30 he decided to set course for Kokura, saying that the other two planes had obviously left the rendezvous point. I tried to persuade him to descend to our scheduled height, but he was adamant that we were better where we were. Wriggling along the tunnel connecting the cockpit to the air-conditioned capsule in the centre of the fuselage was such an effort with a parachute, that I had left it behind. There was no likelihood of our being shot down, and even assuming the worst I had no desire, on a mission such as this, to end up in Jap hands. Hopkins had a brush with me over this, arguing that it was a breach of operational regulations, and we then settled back to our own thoughts.

It was at this point that I had my moment of revulsion, as I believe practically all men called upon to fight a major war do at some time or other. Everything about the flight was different from what I was accustomed to. In Bomber Command we had dressed up in our warmest clothing, to perspire on the ground and, in winter at least, to freeze at operational height in our draughty, unheated aircraft. Here we were two and a half times higher than I had ever been before, sitting in shirt sleeves and comfortably warm. Hardly ever had I done a trip without flak of some kind somewhere in the sky, but here there was none: perhaps three or four bursts which I estimated to be 5,000 feet or more below us. For the first time in my career I was a passenger with no responsibility other than to sit and observe; I would never have believed what a difference this makes. Far below us on the port side was the south-eastern coast of Kyushu, my first sight of mainland Japan. It looked for all the world like the coast of Cornwall, along which I had once flown returning from a difficult raid on Brest and which had then seemed so attractive and welcoming.

The memory brought back another memory, that of the beautiful summer day at school and of sitting under the tree. Suddenly, in my mind, I was a boy once again dreaming of the things I would like to do with my life. And here I was on an errand of death. Around me the others were quietly sitting, just getting on with their job as men and women do the world over, at desks, in the kitchen, on the high seas. For a while I wondered if I would manage to keep myself under control, or collapse under the pressure of two such irreconcilable forces. There were other things that bothered me, too. I hadn't liked the practice sorties that the squadron had been making; they were necessary of course, and there were only four of them, but they had the effect of making the Japanese think there was nothing particularly sinister in this kind of formation at this height. The fact that we were out of range of the defences made me uneasy; it felt unfair. Over Germany we had suffered a permanent casualty rate of just under 5 per cent per night; the average number of trips an aircrew could hope to make was twenty-five. Whatever casualties we might be inflicting – and after all, we argued, the German workers knew we were coming; they could always have abandoned their jobs and fled the cities – we ourselves were suffering proportionately more. In an odd sort of way it felt fair, whereas this did not. Yet this was the mission that was going to cut short the killing by several million, and end the war, perhaps even end all major war. How could one not proceed with it, even though to do so felt like contradicting one's humanity?

When man is brought to an extremity such as this, it cannot be expected that he will be consistent and rational in all his acts. All of us, I believe, contradicted ourselves and said things that we never really meant and later wished we could retract. I know that I did. During a conversation with Tibbetts about the fact that the bomb made another world war impossible, I had impulsively suggested that if by some extraordinary chance the Japanese suddenly surrendered, some kind of demonstration drop ought to be arranged so that people would know just what it meant. He took me to task for it. But it was one of those things you say under stress and do not really mean. On the cruiser Augusta, Truman is reported as having greeted the news of Hiroshima with the words: 'It's the greatest thing in history.' Historians have taken him to task for this and omitted the other things he said, which far more faithfully reflect his true feelings. It has to be said that, whilst man has a duty to take up arms against the aggressor whom nothing else will stop, war carries its own momentum, as do also the instruments that it compels one to use; one ends by taking measures unthinkable at the beginning. From now on the imperative is to make aggression impossible.

We were late reaching Kokura, but found too much cloud for a visual bombing run – 'naked eye or scratch' had been the briefing instruction. There was no sign of the other two aircraft, and the only radio communication had been two words from Sweeney, 'Where's Bock?', clearly an accidental transmission. Hopkins called out, 'Chuck? Is that you, Chuck? Where the hell are you?', but there was no answer, and at 10.00 hours Hopkins set off for the secondary target, Nagasaki. Sweeney's orders had been to wait no longer than fifteen minutes over Yaku Shima but he was a man who liked everything done correctly, and in spite of his fuel problem he circled round in loose formation with Bock, in the 'Great Artiste', only after forty minutes waggling his wings to signal that they were to set course for the target.

At 08.00 a warning light on the black box in Sweeney's aircraft indicated a fault in the bomb. It was far too late to start testing all the circuits, and Ashworth made an intuitive guess; he found and repaired the faulty switches. But Sweeney now had an additional worry. He had done two runs onto Kokura from opposite points of the compass without managing a visual, and when his flight engineer reported the fuel level as dangerously low, he left for Nagasaki, telling his bomb-aimer, Captain Beahan, that they could only afford one run and if there was no visual sighting it would have to be a no drop. The weather on the approach run was even worse than Kokura, and it began to dawn on Sweeney that with no fuel latitude he would have to fly a direct course to Okinawa, the nearest emergency landing field, and jettison the bomb over the first open stretch of sea that was clear of shipping. At 11.00, with the city still visible only on radar, Beahan suddenly shouted: 'I've got it. I see the city. I'll take it now.' One minute later, at 11.01, the bomb dropped, Sweeney went into a rate-four turn to get as far away as possible from the shock waves, and Bock, flying behind him, dropped the instrument capsule in which was Alvarez' record message to Sagani.

For the past twenty minutes we had been staring intently around us looking for the explosion and wondering what on earth could have happened to Sweeney. All we saw was smoke coming from a town, the result of a medium bomber raid, until there was a cry on the intercom and to port we saw a gigantic plume of billowing white smoke. 'Yes, that's it,' I shouted, but I was wrong; it was an incendiary attack on a town of mostly wooden houses. Quite what warned us I am not certain – I think perhaps a fleeting flash – but we all seemed to know as if by instinct, for there was a simultaneous cry and Hopkins swung the nose round to starboard and into line with the flash of light. The ultra-dark glasses we each had round our foreheads to protect our eyes from the blinding light of the bomb were not needed because we were about fifty miles away. By the time I saw it, the flash had turned into a vast fire-ball which slowly became dense smoke, 2,000 feet above the ground, half a mile in diameter and rocketing upwards at the rate of something like 20,000 feet a minute. I was overcome, not by its size, nor by its speed of ascent but by what appeared to me its perfect and faultless symmetry. In this it was unique, above every explosion that I had ever heard of or seen, the more frightening because it gave the impression of having its immense power under full and deadly control. 'Against me', it seemed to declare, 'you cannot fight.' My whole being felt overwhelmed, first by a tidal wave of relief and hope – it's all over! – then by a revolt against using such a weapon. But, I remembered, I had been sent here for a purpose and as best I could I must get on with my job. The cloud lifted itself to 60,000 feet where it remained stationary, a good two miles in diameter, sulphurous and boiling. Beneath it, stretching right down to the ground was a revolving column of yellow smoke, fanning out at the bottom to a dark pyramid, wider at its base than was the cloud at its climax. The darkness of the pyramid was due to dirt and dust which one could see being sucked up by the heat. All around it, extending perhaps another mile, were springing up a mass of separate fires. I wondered what could have caused them all.

William Laurence, who was fifty miles closer, described it far more vividly in *Dawn Over Zero*:

> We watched a giant pillar of purple fire, 10,000 feet high, shoot up like a meteor coming from the earth instead of outer space. It was no longer smoke, or dust, or even a cloud of fire. It was a living thing, a new species of being, born before our incredulous eyes. Even as we watched, a ground mushroom came shooting out of the top to 45,000 feet, a mushroom top that was even more alive than the pillar, seething and boiling in a white fury of creamy foam, a

thousand geysers rolled into one. It kept struggling in elemental fury, like a creature in the act of breaking the bonds that held it down. When we last saw it, it had changed into a flower-like form, its giant petals curving downwards, creamy-white outside, rose-coloured inside. The boiling pillar had become a giant mountain of jumbled rainbows. Much living substance had gone into those rainbows.

We were a silent crew on our way home. I thanked Hopkins for the courtesy of a cockpit seat, and wriggled my way down the tunnel to join Bill in the central compartment. He startled me by suddenly saying: 'That's only the detonator compared with the bomb that is to come.' He meant the hydrogen bomb, but I asked no questions, because it was beyond my comprehension. Foremost in my mind was a growing conviction that Sweeney had missed the aiming point by two miles or more. I wondered how this could have happened with a crew that had been consistently averaging a 200-yard error from 30,000 feet, but I did not yet know the pressures under which Sweeney had been operating. He had left the target immediately after dropping the bomb and crossed the Okinawa coast with one engine dead through lack of fuel. His mayday call for an emergency landing was refused – as happened to me in precisely the same predicament over Linton-on-Ouse in 1941 coming back from Berlin – so he fired all his distress flares and kept coming in on his approach. At dispersal point they found less than 10 gallons in his wing tanks, apart from the 600 he could not use in the bomb bay. It was 12.30. His co-pilot, Lieutenant Charles Albury, went to the chapel and prayed that what they had just done would put an end to the killing.

We, too, had to land on Okinawa because of fuel shortage, but in spite of asking for priority we were kept circling for an hour. When we reached our dispersal point and switched off, a corporal came flying up and yelled out: 'Guess what's happened?'

We said we couldn't.

'They've dropped a second atom bomb.'

Okinawa seemed in a state of semi-chaos. Everywhere was mud; I do not remember ever in my life seeing so much mud. The Americans had finished fighting for the island only seven weeks ago, and already had twenty-four aerodromes built and in full operational use. It was the work of the fabulous Sea Bees, the American equivalent of our Royal Engineers, whom I had seen at work on Tinian building a harbour at a speed and with an inventiveness that completely staggered me. Okinawa was too preoccupied to bother much about unscheduled arrivals, and it was a full hour before we finally staggered through the mud to the mess. The canteen sergeant pounced on us.

'Have you heard the news?', he asked.

'Yes, they've dropped another atom bomb.'

'No, the war's over.' Across the aerodrome there came the sound of firing. 'That's the boys making whoopee,' said the sergeant.

One of the crew said, 'Let's get the hell out of here.' We swallowed our soup as quickly as we could and made tracks for our B29 and Tinian, which we reached at 23.10, half an hour after Sweeney. The war was still on and the firing at Okinawa, we heard, had caused eight casualties.

In Tokyo there followed six days of high drama, on the outcome of which the lives of many millions of people were to depend. Locked in all-out confrontation were the peace party, now substantially strengthened in resolve, and the military dictatorship, the Gumbutsu, itself hardened still further in its refusal to give in. The leaders of the peace party were Togo, the Foreign Minister, and Kido, the Emperor's most trusted advisor. Prime Minister Suzuki probably also wanted peace, but he was old and vacillating, and under the influence of the military.

At 11.00 on 9 August, just as Beahan called out, 'I've got

it now. I see the city', the Big Six were assembling for an emergency session. Suzuki was uncertain what to do and had consulted the Emperor, who told him to accept the Potsdam Declaration. But the meeting was split down the middle and deadlocked. Suzuki, Togo and Navy Chief Yonai argued for surrender; War Minister Anami, Army Chief Umezu and Chief of the Combined Staff Admiral Toyoda refused surrender even if the Emperor was allowed to keep his throne. After three hours the meeting was adjourned, and in the afternoon the full Cabinet met. Here, too, the same deadlock prevailed, argument and counter-argument merely serving to heighten the anger and frustration of the two opposing factions, until at 11 p.m. the meeting broke up. At this point the Emperor intervened: he asked Suzuki to summon an imperial conference, which could be convened only by a consensus of the Cabinet and, since such a consensus would have been unobtainable, Suzuki manoeuvred the members into giving their agreement without their realising what was happening. When they discovered the subterfuge, Toyoda, Umezu and one or two others angrily voiced their indignation; but it was too late, they were already on the Palace steps.

Once again, only this time in the very presence of the Emperor, the two sides fought it out, an unprecedented happening in imperial history. The military not only predominated by virtue of their position, they also held the strongest card. Even if we were to agree to surrender, they said, the army would not obey us: their orders and their code of honour forbid them. The commanders of the Pacific islands retaken by the Americans had ordered their men to fight to the very last drop of blood, and had then almost all committed ceremonial hara-kiri; could the defenders of the home islands betray such an example?

Far away in Batavia, holding onto his life by the slenderest of threads, van der Post expressed the same thought.

There was no nation of that period for whom honour,

however perverted, was so great a necessity as for the Japanese. I was convinced that unless they could be defeated in such a way that they were not deprived of their honour by defeat, there was nothing but disaster for them and for us.

Finally, in the early hours of the morning, Suzuki interrupted the conference; he had never had the courage openly to state his desire for peace, but he now got to his feet, walked up to the throne and deferentially asked His Imperial Majesty to express his wishes. The others were visibly stunned, and received a second shock when, contrary to custom, the Emperor rose to his feet. He started slowly and, when he felt that his listeners knew what was coming, said:

'Ending the war is the only way to restore peace and to relieve the nation of the terrible distress with which it is burdened.'

He had difficulty in controlling his voice; of the others, some sobbed, some sank back with relief, the rest prostrated themselves on the floor.

> It pains me to think of those who served me so faithfully, the soldiers and sailors who have been killed or wounded in far-off battles, the families who have lost all their worldly goods – and often their lives as well – in the air raids at home. It goes without saying that it is unbearable for me to see the brave and loyal fighting men of Japan disarmed. It is equally unbearable that others who have rendered me devoted service should now be punished as instigators of the war. Nevertheless, the time has come when we must bear the unbearable.

After a few more words he left the room. Constitutionally this was not an imperial decision, merely an expression of what the Emperor would do, were he the person to decide. All the same such an unprecedented intervention overawed and influenced those present. But they had been taken by surprise, and the final outcome was still in doubt. The young and even more fanatical military officers had to be reckoned with. Danger could well threaten those who had initiated this move. At the ensuing Cabinet meeting convened at 04.00 hours to formalise what had taken place, all eleven present signed the document recording the proceedings of the conference; but at the insistence of the military, the words, 'so long as it does not prejudice the position of the Emperor' were included. Later that morning, the 10th, Anami found himself unable to carry his officers with him, and orders were issued in his name, but without his approval of the actual text, that the Home Army must continue fighting, 'regardless of whether we end the war or not'. The Cabinet decided that it would be too dangerous to tell the public what the Emperor had decided and, just as had happened after Potsdam, two contradictory statements were released, one stressing the difficulties that the Government was facing, and the other saying fight on.

Bombs were continuing to fall on Japan, the Russians were racing through Manchuria, and rumours of an impending third atomic attack were circulating. The latter were given added edge by a captured American pilot who, knowing nothing about it but under severe interrogation, decided that the safest thing was to 'confess' that these were true and named the target as Tokyo. Togo decided that he must act. He despatched the surrender document through standard diplomatic channels, and, because of the long delay he knew that this would involve, arranged secretly for the text to be broadcast to America in Morse. It was his one hope of evading military censorship and of preserving the life of the operator to whom the transmission was entrusted, and it worked. The message should have been checked, but it was not. The Americans had to satisfy themselves that it was genuine, and they had also to obtain from their allies an agreement of the acceptance note they had drafted. This note reached Tokyo in the early hours of the 11th, Japanese time, and contained the following crucial clauses:

2. From the moment of surrender, the authority of the Emperor and the Japanese government to rule the state shall be subject to the Supreme Commander of the Allied powers who will take such steps as he deems proper to effectuate the surrender terms . . .

5. The ultimate form of the government of Japan shall, in accordance with the Potsdam Declaration, be established by the freely expressed will of the Japanese people.

The Emperor and the peace party accepted this; indeed they were greatly relieved. The military did not; their views were hardening still further, to the point where a group of young disgruntled officers, led by Major Hatanaka, plotted a coup aimed at isolating the Emperor in the palace and assassinating or imprisoning his advisors, as well as Togo. They failed to win Anami over to their side, but Anami, who should have ordered their immediate arrest, gave them only a slight admonition, and then himself tried to talk Umezu into a coup. An army revolt was only just held off. The Emperor resisted the pressure put on by the Chiefs of Staff to reverse his decision, but was unable to weaken their own resolve. The man who finally broke the deadlock was Kido who, though under threat of death and confined to the palace, had been tirelessly working behind the scenes. On the 13th he won over General Anami.

By the morning of the 14th Allied leaflets had dropped on Tokyo giving the full text of the Japanese government's acceptance of Potsdam and the American reply. The hitherto secret negotiations were now in the open, and in consternation Kido and Suzuki persuaded the Emperor to command that an imperial conference be convened. This was an even more extreme departure from imperial procedure than the Emperor's previous interventions and this time, at last, his moving words carried:

. . . the decision I must now make is like the one made by the Emperor Meiji at the time of the Triple Intervention,

when he bore the unbearable and endured the unendurable.
Now I must do it, and together we must unite to build a
peaceful Japan . . . If it is for the good of the people, I am
willing to make a broadcast.

The imperial rescript announcing surrender was recorded
on tape by the Emperor late that evening, a copy made and
both reels locked away in a safe. An unconditional acceptance
of Potsdam was signed, its text radioed to America and the
document sent through diplomatic channels. On hearing of
this Hatanaka launched his intended coup. He shot the
general commanding the Konoye Division, responsible for
guarding the palace, tricked the duty garrison into thinking
he was acting with authority, and ordered them to occupy
and seal off the palace while he searched for the recordings.
His intention was to destroy them, and in the morning to
shoot the Emperor's advisers unless he could talk them into
changing their minds. He never found the recordings, and
at dawn the GOC Eastern Army entered the palace and
ordered the troops out. Hatanaka, though, still had not given
up. He took over the national broadcasting station and
made an abortive attempt to transmit a message to continue
fighting to the people. That an officer of the imperial army
could do such a thing and not even be reprimanded by
the Chiefs of Staff bears its own testimony to the utter
commitment at all levels of command to death rather than
surrender.

How is it, then, that they did surrender? How is it that,
having laid down their arms, they never carried out what
the honour of the imperial army demanded, in keeping with
the example of all other defeated units across the Pacific
islands? There can only be one answer: that the bomb
enabled them to surrender without having to concede military defeat. They could say, and with absolute truth, that
no man can fight the atomic bomb; that, because it was not
to a human enemy that they were surrendering, they could
lay down their arms with honour. This was the argument

that Kido had used to decisive effect in his skilful negotiations, and which the Emperor also used as the central
point in his broadcast to the nation:

> The enemy has begun to employ a new and most cruel bomb,
> the power of which to do damage is indeed incalculable,
> taking the toll of many innocent lives. Should We continue
> to fight, it would result not only in the ultimate collapse and
> obliteration of the Japanese nation, but also it would lead to
> the total extinction of human civilisation. Such being the
> case, how are We to save the millions of our subjects: or to
> atone Ourselves before the hallowed spirits of Our Imperial
> Ancestors? This is why We have ordered the acceptance of
> the provisions of the Joint Declaration of the Powers.

The message was broadcast at noon on 15 August to an
awed public who had never heard the Emperor's voice,
and many of whom listened on their knees. Hatanaka shot
himself; Anami and a few other officers committed hara-
kiri; a kamikaze squadron set off on a final mission without
enough fuel to return, but there is no record of their having
attacked a target; sixteen B29 aircrew were led off one by
one to be shot, but that was about all. The fearsome reprisals
and the mass hara-kiri that had been planned never took
place. Field Marshal Terauchi refused to accept the
surrender, but he carried out none of his threats. The
Emperor sent his brother, Prince Chi-Chi-Bu, to see him
and talk him round. On the 21st Laurens van der Post was
summoned out of his POW camp, driven to the GOC
who announced the surrender and said: 'We Japanese have
decided to switch, and when we switch we switch sincerely.'
In the camp itself the senior officers had been politely
requested, not ordered, to muster the men that very night
for the port of Batavia.

I was at Sacramento air base, California, a desolate enough
place, when the surrender news was broadcast. On the 11th
I had been ordered by Washington to return and give my

report. I was issued with a number one travel priority and put on a plane that was about to leave for San Francisco, after which I would have to fend for myself. They gave me a bunk, but for the first time I couldn't sleep. At Honolulu, where I might have done, a false rumour of peace was broadcast; all drivers on the island strapped their car hooters down with sticking plaster until the batteries went flat, and every ship in port, it seemed, had its siren blowing. Now, two and a half days after leaving Tinian, I was waiting and waiting. My priority turned out to be useless, there were no eastbound scheduled flights and many other people were waiting too. The news broadcast, which was clearly genuine, left me completely emotionless. I asked the control officer if I could go to the canteen and get some coffee; he said I could but that if a flight turned up while I was away I would miss it. So I had to stay where I was. Finally a Dakota turned up. The pilot lined us all up on the tarmac and said: 'We're on the atom run. Sometimes we carry atomic parts, and sometimes we don't. Regulations require that you hand over matches, cigarette lighters and any combustible material.' The others all looked overawed and handed theirs in. I handed mine over too, but with a different kind of look. After two hours of listening to them saying what a great experience it was being on the atom run, I lost control of myself and said, rather loudly, 'I don't believe it.' This earned me the wrath of the entire plane load, all of whom rounded on me and said, 'Who the hell are you to know?', and quite a lot else besides. They were quite right: I should never have said it, and wished I hadn't.

The following morning I reached my room in the Gralyn Hotel on N street, Washington. It was lunch-time at the British Joint Staff Mission, so I lay down for an hour's sleep. When I woke up, the clock said 10.30, and it was broad daylight. I had slept for twenty-two hours.

It was on Churchill's instructions that I had been sent on the mission, but the general election had taken place while

I was waiting at Hamilton Field for the outbound flight, and it was now Attlee to whom I was to report. I had never been to Number Ten before, and I approached the steps with some trepidation. But six weeks had now elapsed, and this had given me time to compose my thoughts. For better or for worse, I knew the three main points that I wanted to make.

1. The atomic bomb is decisive and final. You cannot fight against it and survive as a nation. If both sides have it equally, neither can afford to attack the other; there is military stalemate.
2. It follows that a third world war will be prevented, and world peace preserved, only if the Western Allies possess an adequate atomic arsenal.
3. The key lies not in the atom bomb itself, for the day will soon come when any nation that has the money, and the incentive, will be able to build its own bomb. It lies in the effectiveness of the delivery system. Future delivery systems will take many forms, but the principal will be rockets coming out of space. At all costs Britain should initiate its own space programme.

Mr Attlee listened intently to my first two points, but seemed to lose interest when it came to the subject of space, and the interview terminated.

This last mission accomplished, I felt lost and empty, and asked the RAF for my discharge. They said I was close to a breakdown and put me in a hospital near the Crystal Palace for a fortnight. I think, perhaps, it had all been a bit much for me.

Part II
Reflection
and a Conclusion

4. Christian Perspective

Today, forty years after all this happened, the world has completed the first stage of its advance into the nuclear age. Looking back from this vantage point, what judgement are we to pass on those dark days, and what lessons can we learn for our continuing journey into the unknown, we who are the pioneers of this new phase of history? What we do and what we decide here and now is not just for ourselves, nor is it just for those who are to come after; it is also for those countless millions who have gone before, victims of two world wars, and other minor wars, all within living memory. 'Tell them,' reads the inscription over their grave, 'Tell them, when you return home, that for your tomorrow, we gave our today.' These men, women and even children came from all nationalities; they were driven by the same urge for peace as today's generation; we who are now shaping tomorrow's world stand in their shoes; it is their sacrifice that has won for us the opportunity we now have.

One of our problems is that we live in an ever-specialising world. The rapid advance of knowledge, in all its different forms and disciplines, forces us more and more to specialise on just a small area of the subject we are studying. Yet the individual part has no independent existence of its own; it can be fully understood, and therefore effectively treated, only when seen in its relationship to the whole. Man is continually thinking that he has solved a problem, only to discover that his supposed solution has triggered off an unforeseen, and undesirable, chain reaction. But how is one to succeed in understanding at one and the same time the complexity of the individual part and that of the whole to which it belongs, be it a human being, humanity as a whole, or whatever else? This dialectic, this tension between these two opposite poles, is with us to stay. The nuclear issue poses an added difficulty. Because of the suddenness with which it has burst upon us and the sheer magnitude of its potential threat, we are caught off balance; we are so obsessed with this one problem that we fail to see the broader whole, of which it is a part. This is what happened to me on my journey to Tinian and during the days that followed. My greatest problem was the struggle to bring my imagination and my emotions under control, so as somehow to look at what was happening calmly and objectively.

In my report to Attlee I had said that the key to peace lay in the Western Alliance having an adequate defence capability, but now I was adjusting myself to life as a Christian and I had to consider how having a nuclear defence, or, come to that, any other military defence, is to be reconciled with the fundamental Christian commandment to love. 'You shall love the Lord your God with all your heart, and with all your soul and with all your mind and with all your strength, and your neighbour as yourself.'

Ever since the episode in the Vanity Fair bar I knew that I must look for the Church, but little did I guess how difficult finding the Church would prove to be nor how many avenues I was to walk along before finally succeeding.

Three things stood out in my mind as a result of reading the New Testament. Firstly, Jesus was a man who spoke with an incomparable authority that astonished his listeners and in their view set Him above every other religious teacher. He had the authority of one who has been appointed to speak and act in another's name, and the authority of one who witnesses to what he has seen and experienced. Secondly, He had power from on high such as no other man has had. He had power over the elements, power over the evil spirits, power to cure the incurable, power to forgive sin, power even over death. Thirdly, the kingdom He had come to establish was to be open to all men everywhere who ultimately would be bound together by a unity as real as that which binds the individual parts of the human body.

Therefore the Church which He founded must possess those same characteristics. It must speak with similar authority and certainty, within its appointed brief; it must have power to forgive sin as Jesus did; and it must be a universal Church such as to win the free and meaningful allegiance of all men and women, of all races and nations, adapting itself to the needs of all – the most simple-minded as well as the highest intellectual – and at the same time maintaining a visible head whose authority reflects that of its founder, the man of Nazareth.

All of us tend to see things according to our background and experience. As a pilot learning to fly I knew the importance of authority. I knew that laws, in my case the laws of flight, have to be learned and obeyed. Obedience to the school that had authority and competence to teach the realities of flight was not a servile act or one that detracted from one's dignity. It was the beginning of wisdom and the prerequisite of the freedom of the skies. Any other route can end only in disaster. How then can it be otherwise with religion? If religion is not to do with truth, if it does not shed some sure light on the realities we cannot see, on the destiny that awaits us in the hidden hereafter and what it requires of us in the here and now, on the meaning of suffering and death, on the truths we need to know about that inexpressible mystery whom we call God and who calls us to enter into a saving dialogue with Him, then it was not what I was seeking.

The answer to these questions, which I had been seeking with an increasing urgency but not finding – though once or twice I thought I had – came suddenly and unexpectedly on a warm August night in 1948. The war had given me an urge to work for a world in which peace would be a reality, but my dreams of doing this had not materialised. I felt that I should not mark time any longer and had embarked on a community scheme to help ex-servicemen resettle into civilian life, believing that this would recapture some of the spirit that had held us together in the war years; but that had failed, too, leaving me with a large empty house and a huge pile of debts. Whilst selling the estate off to pay the creditors, I was asked by the local hospital to find alternative accommodation for one of the former members of the community scheme who was dying of cancer. The only accommodation I had been able to find was the old empty house in which I was still living, and now, three months later, I was watching by his deathbed. The hospital had instructed me over the telephone that I was to wait three hours after I thought he had actually died, and then wash the body and put a clean pair of pyjamas on it. The doctor need not be called until the morning.

My problem was how to occupy the three hours. The house had no electricity, and with only an oil lamp I did not feel like moving around more than I had to. My eye was caught by a book lying half-concealed by some papers on the dresser, and I picked it up. It was *One Lord, One Faith*, an account by Monsignor Vernon Johnson of why, as a distinguished and popular Anglican clergyman, he had become a Roman Catholic. From the very first page it struck a chord within me, and by the time the three hours were up I knew that what I had been looking for was the Catholic Church. The reason that gave me this certainty was exactly the same as the one that had convinced me of the reality of God at the Vanity Fair bar episode. It was the certainty that comes, not from the force of reasoning, but from actual living experience, from an awareness of a personal, inner encounter. There is, of course, no voice to hear, no mental image of what has taken place; one just knows there has been an encounter, mysterious and beyond one's power to describe even to oneself, but nevertheless real, the knowledge of which nobody can take away from us by argument or persuasion.

This does not mean that reason had no share in what took place. Indeed the book addressed itself to the very questions that my mind had been asking, and answered them in a way that more than measured up to the expectations aroused in me by the New Testament. Rather it was that the experience originated in a process of reasoning and then transcended the furthest point that reason can reach. The next day I asked the parish priest if he would give me instruction, or whatever was necessary before joining the Catholic Church, but he refused on the grounds that I had made up my mind much too quickly. Finally he relented, and on Christmas Eve he received me into the Church.

I think I expected that from then on making moral judgements would be simple. If the Church is the guardian and teacher of the commandments entrusted to it by Christ, then all that one needs to know in order to make a correct moral judgement, whether to do with one's personal life or with a nuclear weapon, must be found in the Church's moral teaching. This is true; but I was soon to discover that it is we, individually and collectively, who have to apply basic principles and broad precepts to the concrete moral options of daily life, and this proved much more difficult than I had anticipated. To begin with, the principles had to be studied and understood; even more, one had to make them one's own, so that making moral judgements becomes a sort of instinctive thinking, and not just a reference to rules one has learned by heart. Then I discovered that studying morality can never be just an activity of the mind, but has to be accompanied by a genuine effort to live up to the principles one is learning and pondering. The effort of the will enlightens the mind, and the new insights of the mind strengthen the will.

Even in the first simple steps unexpected difficulties appeared. The commandment not to tell a lie, or the one against stealing, for instance, is on the face of it straightforward and unarguable; but a closer look reveals a problem. If you are asked where your wife is by someone who intends to harm her, you are not at moral fault if you throw him off the scent. If the only way that I can save a starving person's life is to take food that belongs to someone else without his permission, the Church teaches that I must take it. Few people would dispute the correctness of your action in either case; but they may not have stopped to ask on what moral grounds they justify it. Is it that not telling the truth, or taking someone else's property, was morally wrong, but is justified because it prevented a much greater wrong from being done? Or was telling an untruth under those particular circumstances not a lie, and taking food not a theft? If the latter, then our terminology is at fault, as is certainly the case in the nuclear debate. 'Lying' should mean something like withholding the truth from someone who has a right to know it, and 'stealing' the taking of property without due or just cause. If the former, then we are saying that when faced with the choice of two evils we are correct in choosing the lesser. That is another way of saying that the end can sometimes justify a morally wrong means. There are moral theologians who say that a decision based on the lesser of two evils is never morally correct, irrespective of the consequences, and that an immoral means may never be used to attain a good end.

I have to say, however, that I cannot bring myself to agree with a moral principle stated in such absolute terms and held as binding in all circumstances. I accept fully that there are some moral absolutes which do not admit exception; I also know the importance of living to the highest moral standard one can. But when it comes to emergency involving risk to human life, the moral reckoning becomes far from simple, for we are sometimes obliged to inflict an injury on another person, simply to save him from an even greater injury. In cases where human life is at stake, I should have thought that the more accurate test of the correctness of one's action is its intended purpose. Am I trying to do what is in the best interests of all those involved in the emergency? Or, to put it differently, does the course of action I have chosen most accord with the commandment to love all my fellow men?

One can reply, of course, that at this level of activity our moral duty is pretty obvious, and that going into these philosophical whys and wherefores is just a distraction. But we shall find that when we come to confront the nuclear issue the very same moral difficulty is there, and we shall be able to deal with it as we should only if we have worked out a viewpoint of our own which we believe in and can defend against opposing opinions.

Moral theologians, in any case, are not all agreed on how ethical difficulties of this kind are morally evaluated, with the result that they can come to quite different conclusions when addressing a genuine moral dilemma. Their way of formulating the more difficult of their propositions is not easily understood if, like me, you do not have a philosophical grounding; but I have come to think that this is perhaps not a bad thing. Were it otherwise, the theologians and the moralists would be doing all the thinking, and we none; and yet it is each single one of us, theologian and non-theologian alike, who has to develop by our own individual efforts a capability for forming correct moral judgements. The responsibility for interpreting into concrete action the high moral principles that the Church, and many others too, holds up to us rests on our shoulders.

One would have thought that to the true believer, sincerely living the Christian life, all this would be easy, especially in the great global issues that threaten the lives of millions of people; but it is not. Our God is really and truly a hidden God; He moves through history, ever faithful to His covenant of love; but His footprints are nowhere to be seen, His ways are inscrutable and ever mysterious. It seems that He wants us to wrestle with the great moral problems of our day, as if doing so were an essential part of building ourselves as individuals into the unique masterpiece that He intends each of us to be, and collectively of attaining the goal for which mankind is destined. On the one hand we are given a Church that speaks with authority given to it from on high, which we must obey or else lose our sense of direction; on the other the moral choices we make must come from our own hearts, as the free expression of a personal attitude of mind which we have worked, reflected and prayed to bring about, each in our own way and within our personal limitations. Squaring up to the new moral dilemmas of the nuclear age is not something that we can do in isolation. It requires that we unite with all our fellow men, of whatever faith or persuasion, in honest and open dialogue, having as our aim the common good of all men the whole world over, and recognising that we cannot force our moral beliefs on them any more than ours have been forced on us.

As for passing judgement on the experience of World War Two, so as the better to determine our future course, you cannot ask if the bomb was justified without first asking if the war was justified, and no judgement on this is possible without asking the most basic question of all: what is the goal for which man is destined, and what are the rules by which to attain it? What, can we say, is the purpose of the immense journey mankind is making, a journey already three million years long or more? Indeed, since man would never have been but for all that preceded him, should we not say that the journey really began four and a half billion years earlier, with the very formation of the earth itself? What a very small fraction of that journey our forty years occupies. Yet, our responsibility is if anything the greater because of the importance and the magnitude of the whole, of which we are a part and which we at this moment in history represent.

In order to find meaning in it all, each of us must search the sources of his own individual faith. My own need is to analyse the scriptures, for these were where I began, and these are shared by all Christians despite the different ways in which we sometimes interpret them. To read scripture with an open and recollected mind is also, according to its own mode, an encounter with the living word of God, who wishes man to know the high calling for which he has been destined:

Then God said, 'Let us make man in our own image, after

our likeness; and let them have dominion over the fish of the sea, and over the birds of the air, and over the cattle, and over all the earth, and over every creeping thing that creeps over the earth.' So God created man in His own image, in the image of God He created him; male and female He created them. And God blessed them, and God said to them, 'Be fruitful and multiply, and fill the earth and subdue it . . .' And it was so. And God saw everything that He had made, and, behold, it was very good.   [Gen. 1:26, 31 RSV.]

Despite the few finds that have yet been made, the fossil record testifies only too vividly how, from his earliest beginnings and with astonishing commitment and flair, man responded to this command. Three million years ago or so, he had taught himself to manufacture stone tools, using techniques which he can communicate to other groups of hominids, and which take varying forms according to different ages and areas of the world.

He is clearly a compulsive traveller, ever reaching out from the familiar to the unfamiliar, for he is found in Africa, Palestine, the Far East and China. A million years ago there are traces of him in the frozen north. What a prodigious achievement that was. It means that he had found a way of carrying fire along with him and of being certain that he could keep it alight, unless he already knew how to light it himself in the midst of snow.

From the beginning of recorded history it is the same story: a ceaseless quest to lift himself to higher levels of self-realisation, and to gain greater control of the environment in which he lives. Nothing that he can reach or discover is left untouched; he burrows deep into the earth, descends to the bottom of the oceans, searches the outer regions of space. Technology, allied to his power to think and organise, is the instrument through which he achieves this. As age has succeeded age, technology has reached new heights, and new sources of energy and power have been harnessed, of which fire was the first and the atom the most recent. Man cannot live without power, let alone extend his mastery over the created world, but all forms of power carry their dangers. Today fire has been in the essential service of man for something like a million years, but it still manages to elude our control, or is used with malice, and when this happens, it turns into a destroyer of men. Early man, who lived in the dry and hot areas of the world, and who sometimes started bush fires to drive otherwise elusive animals into narrow gorges where he could trap them, must have found it a treacherous and fearsome weapon indeed. Man still suffers grievously at the hands of fire, yet we see it as our friend and our ally, one to be treated with respect and to be kept within bounds, but still our friend; this is also the case with oil, gas, electricity, high explosives and other forms of energy that serve the common good of mankind.

What, then, are we to say of nuclear power? Is it the final source of energy to fall under man's grasp, or are there further elemental forces yet to be harnessed? We do not know. What we are finding out is that life on earth is influenced by the entire universe, of which it forms but a very small part, to an extent that we had previously never dreamed, and that control of the environment in which we live is crucial to our future well-being. Sooner or later our successors may well find that they have an approaching ice age to fend off; if they do not succeed, half of the world will be overwhelmed and the other half be incapable of sheltering and feeding the vast influx of refugees that would result. Are we to deny them the one source of energy that might serve to avert that catastrophe? Without a doubt space will be colonised, and this, too, will call for huge resources of energy and sophisticated technology, and, in addition, some form of policing, for wherever man settles in any significant numbers the policeman is needed. These considerations, and others like them, have to be taken into account in the decisions we need to make here and now.

The primordial revelation, 'Fill the earth and subdue it', did not disclose the whole of God's plan for mankind.

Having spoken down the ages in many and various ways, God was finally to speak with His own voice through a Son, His only begotten and beloved Son, Jesus Christ, whom He sent on a mission to man as an active, decisive participant in human history. In Him God's revelation to man was completed, and His hidden plan for mankind finally disclosed:

> He has made known to us in all wisdom and insight the mystery of His will for us, according to His purpose which He set forth in Christ as a plan for the fullness of time, to unite all things in Him, things in heaven and things on earth. [Eph. 1:9.]

These words I find mysterious and profoundly moving, because of the new light they shed on the ultimate unity that God intends for the entire creation. For me it was the experience of war that first opened my eyes to the oneness of our human family, and helped me see the extent to which we all depend upon each other, in countless unseen and unnoticed ways, from the very top down to the person who does the most ordinary and simple job. Looking back on those years, I still marvel at the way the awareness of facing a common danger and of striving for a common goal enkindled in men's hearts an *esprit de corps,* a unity of purpose, a sense of dependence upon one another, which gave a new dimension to the human spirit. Man did not need to be told that on the quality of his work, however humble it might be, depended the well-being of others and the attainment of the goal for which all were struggling, and that his own personal good was inextricably linked with the good of others. It is a sad reality that in time of full-scale war, which of its nature is evil, man goes to such lengths of sacrifice for what he considers to be the common good; and that in time of peace, which in essence is good, he retreats back into the more limited world of his own private interests and hopes, without seeing that he himself is thereby the loser. For it is precisely by becoming more involved with mankind as a whole and less with his immediate circle that man finds inner fulfilment and attains to the full stature of perfection for which he is destined.

The unity which God's creation will ultimately achieve, and the rôle that man has been given in bringing that about, is a central theme of the New Testament. It rings out in the sublime prayer that Jesus offered on our behalf immediately before His passion and death on the cross:

> That they may all be one; even as thou, Father, art in me, and I in thee, that they also may be in us. I in them and thou in me, that they may become perfectly one, so that the world may know that thou hast sent me and hast loved them even as thou has loved me.   [John 17:11,21.]

In the person of Jesus Christ, who is truly God and yet also truly man, the uncreated and the created are now forever united. The invisible God who lives in inapproachable light, wholly other than man and wholly transcendent, has taken to Himself our very own human nature, and by this act of adoption given us a share in His own divine nature. Originally commanded to master the earth, and bring harmony and coherence into its constituent parts, we have now been appointed co-creators with Him of the new heaven and the new earth, foreseen and planned from all eternity as our future and lasting home. Between these two creations, the old and the new, there is an absolute difference and yet also a real continuity in the same kind of way that the flower differs from the seed, yet is organically one and the same. We, in our here-and-now, in the fulfilment of our duties and our enterprises, in the good we do and the patience we show in our daily trials, in a multiplicity of unsuspected ways, are participating in that mysterious and marvellous process whereby the seed we plant in the ground, there to die, finally becomes a flower.

Our beautiful world, torn as it is by so many divisions

and confrontations – by wars, by injustices, by poverty of the most extreme kind – may well seem to contradict this high and noble calling. We may well ask how it is possible in one and the same breath to hold up such a vision of man's destiny and to justify going to war against an unjust aggressor, let alone dropping an atomic bomb on a fellow human being's city. This is the desperate cry that has sounded forth from the human heart down the ages of human history and will continue so to sound until all is finally consummated; how explain the seemingly irreconcilable opposites of a loving God and a world filled with suffering? In the same epistle that St Paul describes God's hidden and loving plan in such moving terms, he sheds some light on this darkness:

> For we are not contending with flesh and blood, but against the principalities, against the powers, against the world rulers of this present darkness, against the spiritual hosts of wickedness in the heavenly places. Therefore take the whole armour of God that you may be able to stand in the evil day.   [Eph. 6:12,13.]

Here, in part, is revealed the reason for the many evils that beset the human family, and which impede our forward march towards the goal of our ultimate destiny. We find within ourselves a clash of opposites, a tension between Good and Evil, so that 'the things that we would we do not do, and the things that we would not we do.' Amongst us we have an enemy, bent on turning us away from the narrow path that will alone lead us through the dangers of the nuclear age, the enemy of whom C.S.Lewis in his *Screwtape Letters* wrote so vividly. This is an added reason for our conducting this crucial moral debate in a spirit of mutual understanding and with all the honesty of thought we can muster. There is no room for trying to score points or for casting doubts on each other's motives; for we are all involved, we will all fall if we get it wrong, just as we will be the winners if we get it right.

5. Morality of Defence

We live in a pluralist society, in which men and women brought up in diverse cultures, religions and ideological convictions see life and its purpose from widely differing perspectives. This variety of background and thought-process is reflected to an even greater extent in the world around us, in one sense enriching our common humanity, in another provoking misunderstanding and confrontation. How, amid such diversity of views, are we to arrive at morally correct norms of behaviour which the majority of men will accept, and in particular how are we to agree on the rights and wrongs of armed defence in the nuclear age?

We may differ in the view we take of the purpose of life and of where history is leading, but we all agree that society cannot function harmoniously without the rule of law. From the very earliest beginnings, all communities of men found the need to establish norms of behaviour which were considered binding on its members and reinforced by some form of sanction. Hence the Latin *mores*, from which the term morality derives. Later these norms, or customs, became enshrined in the codified systems of law, whose quality and ethical standard played a decisive rôle in forming the nation's character. Israel, for instance, stood head and shoulders above her far more cultured and sophisticated neighbours by virtue of the Mosaic Law, given to her during her difficult, and often rebellious, forty-year journey through the Sinai desert.

Law may be defined as an ordinance of reason made for the common good and promulgated by the person, or persons, responsible for the particular society, be it a small grouping, the nation or mankind as a whole. The purpose of law is to maintain order, predictability and justice in human affairs, and to enable society to achieve its particular end. The better the law and the more faithfully it is kept, the greater the harmony, and the more effectively society can achieve its goal. Conversely, bad law perverts the cause of justice and disrupts harmony. To break the law is to introduce some measure of disorder into society. Systematic, large-scale law-breaking leads society towards anarchy, and anarchy is such a frightening condition that men are willing to accept dictatorship rather than endure it. This is why anarchy is deliberately brought about by those who wish to impose a despotic or totalitarian rule upon others. At superficial levels of social life, for instance with the highway code, all this is self-evident; no reasonable man questions the need for a common and binding rule of the road, or complains that being forced to drive on the left rather than where he will is an infringement of his personal liberty. How should it be different, then, with the roadway of life?

When man was created in the image of God, and in the fullness of time told of the eternal destiny that awaited him, he was not left without the means of knowing the way he must take to achieve it. For this he could never even remotely know by the light of human reason alone. Just as the material creation had been given physical laws to hold its many diverse elements together, in a marvellous and self-complementing harmony, and orientated towards an even more marvellous process of evolution, so man was given moral and spiritual laws appropriate to his nature and essential to the fulfilment of his destiny. How is it, then, one may well ask, that if so much hangs on knowing and keeping these laws, there is such confusion and controversy as to what they are, or even if they exist at all?

Man, as unifier of the entire creation, visible and invisible, was called at one and the same time to walk by faith and to exercise the full use of reason, his feet on earth and his head in heaven. As scripture put it, man walked in the presence of God, in a free and friendly dialogue; but early on something went badly wrong, and this happy relationship was broken:

> Now the serpent was more subtle than any other wild creature that the Lord God had made. He said to the woman, 'Did God say, "You shall not eat of any tree of the garden"?' And the woman said to the serpent, 'We may eat of the fruit of the trees of the garden; but God said, "You shall not eat of the tree which is in the midst of the garden, neither shall you touch it, lest you die." ' But the serpent said to the woman, 'You shall not die. For God knows that when you eat of it your eyes shall be opened, and you will be like God, knowing good and evil.' So when the woman saw that the tree was good for food, and that it was a delight to the eyes, and the tree was to be desired to make one wise, she took of the fruit and ate; and she also gave some to her husband, and he ate.
>
> Then the eyes of both were opened, and they knew that they were naked; and they sewed fig leaves together and made themselves aprons.
>
> And they heard the sound of the Lord God walking in the garden in the cool of the day, and the man and his wife hid themselves from the presence of the Lord God among the trees of the garden. But the Lord God called to the man, 'Where are you?' And he said, 'I heard the sound of Thee in the garden, and I was afraid, because I was naked; and I hid myself.' He said, 'Who told you that you were naked? Have you eaten of the tree of which I commanded you not to eat?' The man said, 'The woman whom Thou gavest to be with me, she gave me fruit of the tree, and I ate.' Then the Lord God said to the woman, 'What is this that you have done?' The woman said, 'The serpent beguiled me and I ate.' [Gen. 3:1–12.]

What a familiar and revealing account handed down by early man of the way we fall into sin! Adam puts the blame on his wife, and she on the serpent. They both have a guilty conscience and try to conceal what has happened. The serpent, that master of deceit, Satan, is too clever for them.

He starts by falsifying the facts, so as to present God in an unfavourable light. Not all the fruit in the garden had been forbidden, only that of one tree. When Eve corrects the mistake, he resorts to an outright lie, 'You will not die. . . . You will be like God', and goes on to the monstrous accusation that God commanded them not to eat only so as to prevent them from becoming equal to Himself. Satan was formerly Lucifer, the Archangel of Light, so consumed by the thought of his own beauty and magnificence that he refused his creator the honour and service due to Him, with the words, 'I will not serve.'

> Now war arose in heaven, Michael and his angels fighting against the dragon; and the dragon and his angels fought, but they were defeated and there was no longer place for them in heaven. And the great dragon was thrown down, that ancient serpent, who is called the Devil and Satan, the deceiver of the whole world – he was thrown down to earth, and his angels were thrown down with him. [Rev. 12:7–9.]

Satan struck at Adam and Eve's most vulnerable point, the juncture between faith and reason, and, we can infer, at a critical moment in their lives, perhaps while they were making up their minds how to set about the task they had been given. We do not know what precisely it was they were forbidden; we know only that the basic temptation was to become their own arbiters of what is right and wrong, and their own architects of the future. The temptation in the garden of Eden has its parallel, and its reversal, in Jesus's confrontation with Satan, after he had been baptised in the Jordan by John.

> Then Jesus was led by the Spirit out into the wilderness to be tempted by the Devil. He fasted for forty days and forty nights, after which He was very hungry and the tempter came and said to Him, 'If you are the Son of God, tell these stones to turn into loaves.' [Matt. 4:1–3.]

The temptation is powerful and very real, Jesus is the Messiah, and on the fulfilment of His mission depends the fate of mankind. It has needed forty days of solitary, continuous prayer to discover and accept how His Father wants Him to carry out this momentous task, and the Spirit is still keeping Him in the desert. He is now in a critical position, cut off from help, too weak to get back to human habitation, and becoming weaker. The tempter points out that there is an easy solution, the only possible solution. Just one word, and these stones will turn into bread. One can almost picture the words: 'Otherwise you will die, here in the desert, a failed Messiah. You know, after all, that God helps those who help themselves.' This was a compelling appeal to reason, but it meant disobeying God. Jesus had been led by the Spirit into the desert and must remain there until the Spirit was ready to send Him out. 'Man shall not live by bread alone but by every word that proceeds from the mouth of God.' [Matt. 4:4.]

Two millennia previously, in his supreme hour of trial, Abraham had responded in a similar way:

> After these things God tested Abraham, and said to him, 'Abraham!' And he said, 'Here am I.' He said, 'Take your son, your only son Isaac, whom you love, and go to the land of Moriah, and offer him there as a burnt offering.' . . .
>
> Then Abraham put forth his hand, and took the knife to slay his son. But the angel of the Lord called to him from heaven, and said, 'Abraham, Abraham.' And he said, 'Here am I.' He said, 'Do not lay your hand on the lad or do anything to him; for now I know that you fear God, seeing you have not withheld your son, your only son, from me. [Gen. 22:1–12.]

We are told very little about Jesus's trial; but that in his case, too, help arrived only at the very last moment can be inferred from the fact that when the Devil finally left: 'angels appeared and ministered to him' (Matt. 4:11.). To have needed the help of angels, He must have been at the last extremity of life.

Dare one suggest that the words of the angel who stayed the hand of death as it was about to strike were similar to those spoken to Abraham? 'Now I know that you fear God, seeing that you did not withold your life, your only life, from me.'

Adam and Eve, in their very different circumstances, must also have found themselves in some form of dire quandary, their mission in jeopardy and the situation retrievable only by taking affairs into their own hands, at the expense of some commandment given to them by God. Come to think of it, what an attractive prospect, what a feeling of power: being able to shape the future according to one's own ideas! What independence and security, being one's own arbiter of right and wrong! Here was the *'non serviam'*, the 'I will not serve', of Lucifer repeated by man, and in its immediate consequences equally catastrophic. The guiding, loving hand of God had been rejected, and without it the human family had no hope of knowing the way to Heaven, let alone lifting itself up to that new order of existence.

By believing Satan rather than God, Adam and Eve opened the door that guarded the heart of man and allowed the Devil to enter. He was no longer a distant and recognisable adversary, but a hidden, subversive infiltrator within the human fold, free to roam, like a poisonous virus that infects and debilitates. From now on he would prey on human weakness; disorganise, spread confusion and misunderstanding; fan the flames of human discord into open warfare; do all in his power to divide men from each other and from God. Against God Himself he can do nothing, for God has no adversary. Satan's contest is with man, and with the carrying out of God's plan for him. His first success has been to make it unfashionable, even a little ridiculous, to believe that he exists at all; his second to have deadened man's sense of sin. Sin is not really something that one talks about; it is embarrassing and in bad taste. For in the contemporary view everything is all right so long as we are not harming other people; the rest is a matter for the individual to decide himself. But sin is the door, in fact the only door, through which Satan can enter our hearts and gain power over us. The mind has a primary duty to stand guard over the heart, to challenge the suggestions and the thoughts that seek entry and allow them in only if they have a rightful place. Once inside, as in the case of giving in to fear in time of danger, great strength will be needed to throw them out.

Since the Devil cannot deny or impede God, his attack is against man's acceptance of God's loving plan. He wants to conceal God, to make man picture Him as other than He really is. The God who lives in unapproachable light and yet also dwells mysteriously and lovingly within the heart of man is a profound mystery indeed, beyond the power of man to comprehend. The more man can be made to see Him as either solely transcendent and inaccessible, and therefore not involved in the daily affairs of the world, or solely indwelling, and not wholly other than His creation, the better. The less relevant to the problems of the modern age God will then appear to be, and the more readily will man dispense with faith and decide those issues by the light of reason alone.

This is a pitfall that we all have to try and avoid in our search for the narrow road that offers a way through the moral dilemma of nuclear weapons. But this is one dilemma which admits of no wholly satisfactory answer. Whichever of the available options we choose, and it appears to me that there are basically only two, we are left with considerable moral problems, not to mention military and political difficulties.

I take as my starting point the fundamental question: do nations have the right of armed self-defence against unlawful and armed aggression? For on the view we take of this much will depend on the nuclear debate.

The right of self-defence has been assumed from the beginning of recorded history, and consistently upheld by the Christian Church. Only the absolute pacifist rejects it. The Law of Nations sees international society as consisting of a series of sovereign states, each of which has certain basic rights, the principal of which are territorial integrity and political sovereignty. International law upholds the inviolability of these two rights, grants the victim state the right to defend itself, and permits other states to come to its aid. The major crime against international society is stated to be aggression, but once again we are faced with the problem of poverty of terminology. Whereas on the domestic scene violation of the individual's right to be secure in his own house and, within the law, to manage his family affairs in his own way, is categorised according to degree – such as trespass, theft, burglary, and so on – in international law aggression is the only term. A further complicating factor is the increasing tendency to manipulate words: every aggressor is always a 'peace-maker' who will go to great lengths to be allowed to occupy the other's territory unimpeded and in the guise of a liberator.

There is no policeman on the international scene; the victim, with those willing to help him, has to act as his own policeman. This, too, compounds the problem, for, however hard we may try, none of us are wholly just and objective when deciding our own cause. Other nations, subjected as they will be to intense diplomatic lobbying, may disagree with us. Yet, act as policeman we have to; and this not only because our own survival as a free nation is at stake, but because resisting an aggressor has a moral value in itself. The common values of international society are strengthened when aggression is resisted, and diminished when, either through appeasement or capitulation, it is allowed to triumph. For the very reason that there is no policeman to protect the rights of nations, aggression in the international field is much more dangerous than is domestic violence. International law confers the right, indeed the duty, not only to resist the aggressor but, once he is defeated, to insist on due restitution and reparation, and if necessary, to punish him in order to deter potential future aggressors. The under-lying moral issue is the same as with terrorists, hijackers, kidnappers and the like: experience as well as reason tells us that they have to be resisted and brought to justice, or else the floodgates will open.

Consider the relative actions of Britain and Finland in the run-up to World War Two. Britain was a world power, holding herself up as a champion of freedom and justice. Had she decided to stand by Czechoslovakia, the combined Allied armies would have outnumbered Hitler's, yet she adopted a policy of appeasement. There were undoubtedly extenuating circumstances, and there are those even today who defend her action; but no one thinks well of her for having chosen the course of safety rather than honour. Finland, on the other hand, a small nation, without a single effective ally, was handed an ultimatum by Russia demanding substantial territorial concessions under threat of invasion. She had no conceivable hope of withstanding the armed might of the Soviet Union, but she decided to fight rather than capitulate, and as a result conceded considerably less than the original demand, and earned the respect and admiration of the international community.

So far, it would appear, so good. If nations have the right to self-defence against an unlawful aggressor, and if the exercise of that right contributes to the stability and the values of international society, what is now required is to discover the extent to which nuclear weapons affect that right. However, first it is necessary to examine the claim of pacifism which denies the right of armed defence altogether. It is a view which with the advent of nuclear weapons has attracted a growing number of adherents, and on which each of us must make a personal and informed judgement.

Pacifist is a term that has many connotations and is used in many different senses. In its loosest sense it may be taken as indicating a lover of peace who works to the utmost of his ability to achieve a peaceful solution, and according to this interpretation the great majority of men can be called pacifists. In its strict sense it denotes a rejection of war as a means of settling disputes between nations, but in practice there are varying views as to how this fundamental tenet of faith should be interpreted. At one end of the spectrum stand the absolute pacifists, who hold that there are no circumstances under which it is morally permissible to take another person's life. Amongst these there are some who seek to propose an alternative form of defence against an armed invader, and others who offer no alternative but merely say that it is better to be overwhelmed than to resist. At the other end of the spectrum is the conditional pacifist who grants sovereign states the right of armed defence, but strictly limits the type of weapon that may be used and the targets that may be attacked.

There are also, of course, those who embrace pacifism merely because they do not want to find themselves in the firing line, just as there are others who, while refusing to fight out of deep personal conviction, willingly place themselves in the thick of the fighting, for instance as medical orderlies. Of these differing forms, it is absolute pacifism, which denies the state any use of armed force, no matter what the circumstances or even the consequences, that concerns us at the moment. If this can be clearly shown as being in the best interests of mankind as a whole, and as more perfectly fulfilling the commandment to love our neighbour, then no armed defence, let alone a nuclear one, should be permitted to the nation.

There is no denying that this point of view, radical and extreme though it undoubtedly is, holds a strong attraction for many people, particularly amongst the young. Most of us feel an instinctive horror at the thought of having to kill a fellow human being, and we know that to lead our lives in the way we should means loving our neighbour. Pacifism directs its appeal to the law of love implanted in every human heart. It claims that we have a duty to work for the good of our enemies, however brutal or evil they may be, and that we may never kill them. The Christian pacifist will point to the example of Christ who offered his life as a sacrifice for mankind, thereby fulfilling to the bitter end the law of love that he had consistently preached; he will argue that Evil is not overcome by physical force but rather by sacrifice and love. He will also say that the policy of armed defence has not succeeded in preventing war; on the contrary, wars are if anything becoming more frequent, therefore it is high time that a different response was tried. By these and other similar arguments he is able to mount what to many will appear a convincing case based on a lofty and spiritual ideal. However it is one thing to formulate an ideal in the abstract, another to give it relevance to our duties as members of the human family, and still another to show that, stated in such absolute terms, it adequately fulfils the commandment to love our fellow men as ourselves.

The specifically Christian pacifist makes appeal to scripture in support of his belief that killing is never morally justified. Before examining this appeal, one fundamental point needs to be made. There are some Christian sects who regard scripture as the sole source of Christian belief, to be interpreted in an individual way. But the New Testament was written by the early Church, and pronounced as being canonical many years after the death of Christ. Therefore it is the Church standing in the line of apostolic succession to Peter and the other apostles that is the guardian and the interpreter of scripture. If it is true that the Church's teaching must not contradict the clear meaning of scripture, it is also true that scripture and the teaching tradition of the Church have to be seen as forming an integral whole. Further, in appealing to scripture one cannot take just one quotation to prove a particular point, if doing so is inconsistent with the teaching of scripture as a whole. There are many apparent paradoxes in the Bible, whose authors were writing for a contemporary audience and whose literary style and form often conveys a different sense now than intended and understood at the time.

There is no doubt that the Gospel preached by Jesus is

at heart one of love and reconciliation. He had come to free man from the power of sin and death, and thereby to reconcile man and God. But the very nature of His mission involved a spiritual warfare which placed him in open confrontation with the forces of Evil, and was to result in persecution and violent death, for others as well as himself. Inevitably this would lead to many paradoxes, even apparent contradictions, in his life and teaching, leaving us with no clear formula for all the complexities of human affairs. He preached 'turn the other cheek', but forcibly drove the moneychangers out of the temple and overturned their tables. The peace he spoke of was not such as the world gives, for he said: 'Do not think I have come to bring peace on earth; I have come not to bring peace, but a sword.' (Matt. 10:34.) He uses the analogy of going to war to reinforce a particular precept; he foretells that nation will fight nation; but he has nothing to say about the right of nations to defend themselves. If this age-old, universally assumed right were from now on to be revoked, with all that this would involve for international society, one would expect that He would have told us.

The Gospel abounds with the call to place ourselves at the service of God and our neighbour, and to live our lives in a spirit of love and sacrifice. There is nothing greater we can do than to lay down our life on behalf of someone else. If it is a question of my assailant's life or his, and other people's lives do not depend on my preserving mine, the counsel of perfection is to offer mine rather than take his. But when other people are at risk, not just me, the position is very different. We cannot easily conclude one way or the other from its general theme what scripture has to say about this.

There is the commandment, 'You shall not kill'. But this was promulgated in the Old Testament, and cannot have been meant in an absolute sense; but only as applying to what we term manslaughter or culpable homicide or murder. Otherwise how can one explain the military campaigns which

God told the Israelites to undertake and which, because of the way He intervened on their behalf, were seen as compelling proofs of His love for His chosen people? To argue that the ten commandments forbade the nation to go to war is to make nonsense of whole sections of the Old Testament. One may claim that the New Covenant changed all this; it did indeed, but by bringing the old to completion, by giving it a profound and spiritual dimension such as had never been envisaged, not by contradicting it. There is nothing in the New Testament that denies nations the right to maintain armies. The text that bears most directly upon the right of the state to be armed is where the soldiers ask John the Baptist what they should do, and he answers, 'no intimidation, no extortion, be content with your pay'. When contrasted with his outright condemnation of the Pharisees this clearly indicates that he does not see the fact of their being soldiers as contrary to the will of God: it is not credible that in a matter of such moment and on so solemn an occasion the Baptist should have failed to tell us if it were. Appeal is also made to Jesus's instruction to Peter at the time of his arrest in Gethsemane:

> Put your sword into its sheath; shall I not drink the cup which the Father has given me?. . .For all those who take the sword will perish by the sword. Do you think that I cannot appeal to my Father, and He will at once send me more than twelve legions of angels? [John 18:11; Matt. 26:53.]

But this cannot be taken as a denial of the nation's right to maintain an armed police and defence force to keep the peace, discourage crime and anarchy, and to protect fundamental human rights. Peter was acting in a private capacity against the authorised police of the state. One may also ask how, if a sword is never to be used, Peter was allowed to carry one. The Gospel evidence is weighted far more in favour of the right of nations to police and defend themselves than against it, and the epistles, full as they are of military metaphors, even more so.

Another line of argument is that, until the Emperor Constantine Christianised the Roman Empire in 303, the early Church was pacifist. Only with the corrupting effect of participation in the affairs of state that this dramatic change brought about did she lose her pristine purity of faith. But this involves reading more into the history of the first three centuries than the facts justify, and is a strongly contested assertion. The early Christians were a small, severely persecuted community which in its formative years appears to have looked upon the end of the world as imminent. That a prohibition was placed upon becoming a Roman soldier is undoubtedly true, though to what extent is not quite certain. Rome was the Church's principal enemy, and service with the Roman army involved certain obligations which were incompatible with Christianity, as for instance Emperor worship. The Christian community was allowed no part in public affairs, and may well have seen little point seeking an army career. What is clear is that after Constantine's conversion the prohibition on military service was lifted, and ever since the Church has consistently upheld the basic right of self-defence. Even if one were able to demonstrate that the primitive Church believed pacifism to be a fundamental stance required by the Gospel, it still would not follow that the Church was right for the first three centuries and wrong for the subsequent seventeen. Earlier as against later is not a criterion for correctness of moral judgement for the Church, commissioned to teach in the name of Christ until the end of time. The early Church was not always able to solve its moral dilemmas, as for instance that of slavery, the condemnation and abolition of which were left to later generations.

The absolute pacifist bases his case on the belief that there are no circumstances under which it is lawful intentionally to take another person's life; that is, the police may no more kill than may the army. Extreme though it is, this view has the merit of applying the same standard to the domestic problem of law and order as to the international one of war, and thus acknowledges that the basic moral issue is the same in the one as in the other. Let us, then, invoke the domestic analogy and begin with a simple act of terrorism such as happens in our contemporary world. This, I find, is the logical entry into the nuclear debate; it means that one can isolate and clarify the basic principles that govern the morally correct use of force, and then proceed step by step to see how those principles stand up to the ever-increasing pressure of modern weaponry.

Let us suppose that three of the 200 passengers in the customs hall of an airport have taken sub-machine-guns out of their luggage and are opening fire on the other passengers, as happened some years ago at Tel Aviv Airport. There is an armed policeman on duty who has not yet been noticed and who is in a position to shoot the gunmen. Because of the distance between him and them, this is his only way of stopping them. How does he properly fulfil his duty to love his fellow men? To be loyal to his belief, the pacifist must deny the policeman the right to shoot, if so doing risks killing one of the gunmen. In practice, however, I find that this is one question to which he is loathe to give a direct answer. If he says that the morally correct course of action is to shoot, he has abandoned his position as an absolute pacifist to become a conditional pacifist, and agrees that there are circumstances under which the right of armed defence does exist. He may claim that these are extremely limited, but at least he concedes that they can exist, and if they exist on the domestic scene it is difficult to argue that they may not also exist on the broader international scene. If on the other hand he says that the policeman may not shoot, he is almost certain to lose credibility with those listening to the discussion. In my own experience I have hardly ever known an absolute pacifist give a categoric yes or no in reply to this question. Occasionally someone will say that he has wrestled with this very problem and simply does not know what the solution is. Other answers I have heard are: 'I'd need to know a lot more about their motives'; 'Perhaps they could be talked out of it'; 'I would charge at them'; 'Why ask such a stupid question?'

The question the Christian has to answer is: how, and according to what principles of interpretation, does the precept to love our enemies apply in the context we are postulating? Unless we can arrive at an unequivocal and competent judgement on the policeman's moral duty in this simple case, we can hardly hope to speak with authority on the complex and difficult issue of all-out war between major powers.

The policeman, whose legal and moral duty is to maintain law and order, has only two options: he can either shoot and so halt the massacre, or he can refrain from shooting and allow the massacre to continue. Either way there will be blood on his hands: the blood of 200 innocent people if he fails to stop the killing, the blood of three guilty men if he does stop it. He cannot opt out of the situation on the plea that the crisis is not of his making, for he is an integral part of it, by virtue of his office and the fact that he has the power to stop the massacre. So long as he fails to exercise that power he makes himself to some degree a contributor to the crime being perpetrated, albeit an extremely unwilling one. In seeing the commandment, 'You shall not kill', as an absolute prohibition which makes the shooting of the gunmen an inadmissible moral option, the pacifist stands alone. Almost all moralists, religious as well as secular, hold that in such a situation, where no other way exists of stopping the massacre that is taking place, the commandment to love one's fellow men can be translated into action only by shooting the perpetrators of the crime. He is not using an immoral means to achieve a good end, because shooting the criminal is not, under these circumstances, an immoral action. A murderer, whilst in the process of committing murder, forfeits his right to have his life protected by the law so that he may complete his murderous work.

This, however, is a simple, black and white case. Let us add a further and complicating dimension. The gunmen have seized a ten-year-old boy from the customs hall and are using him as a human shield. What is the policeman's duty now? If he can shoot the gunmen with a high degree of probability of not killing the boy, the moralists hold that the policeman has the same duty as in the first case. However, if the probability is the other way round, the moralists become divided. One school says that the policeman's duty is now reversed: he may not shoot through the boy in order to kill the gunmen, on the grounds that the boy is innocent, that to kill him would be immoral, and that an immoral means may never be used to achieve a good end. I have wrestled with this argument, but have to say that I find it unsatisfactory; it leaves me with an uneasy conscience, and the reasoning does not convince me. If it were the only line of moral thinking in the Church, I suppose I would be in difficulty, my conscience opposing what the teaching Church teaches. But mercifully it is not.

At the heart of the issues lies the precept that a good end cannot justify an immoral means. The proposition, I feel, is wrongly formulated, for a great deal does depend on the nature of the end, on that of the means, and on the funda-mental intention behind the act. To use the words of a well known Jesuit moral theologian, it seems to me that 'circumstances do change cases'. This does not mean that circumstances decide morality. Not at all. But circum-stances, as well as the probable consequences of the options open to us, do come into the moral reckoning. To walk past a boy dying of thirst with a bucket of water in one's hand and not to give him any would in most people's judgement be a morally unacceptable act. But suppose the area is drought-stricken and my reason for ignoring the boy is that I need the water for those who, if they can be revived, look the most able to help me find more water. Withholding the means of life is a different thing from actually taking life, but the predicament in which we both find ourselves is basically the same. Of course there are other questions to be asked. Why did I not come better equipped? Or arrive sooner? What is the world community doing? But these are not relevant for the moment, any more than the airport security lapse, or Britain's political failure in the thirties, was relevant once the shooting had started. Both the policeman and I have a crisis on our hands. In a crisis such as this, where one has power to let some die in order that others may live, every second's delay may be yet another life lost. Neither the policeman nor I can be sure of the outcome of our actions. He is faced with a struggling, moving target; the hall is full of screams, gunfire and panic. He may kill the boy, miss the gunmen and be shot himself before he can fire again, or he may manage to miss the boy and save the remaining passengers, just as my little boy dying of thirst may still be rescued if help can be organised quickly enough. Yet, according to one moral school, somewhere along the spectrum of probability lies a point beyond which the policeman's morally good act becomes a morally bad act. But by what moral principle is this to be judged? The policeman's markmanship, his ability to remain calm under stress, the boy's movement between the instant of the trigger being pulled and the bullet arriving, are all determining factors of the outcome. Further, if it is morally wrong to shoot when to do so jeopardises the little boy's life, it must also be wrong to resist the kidnapper who looks like shooting his hostage if his demands are not met. Kidnappers would then know that they only had to be sufficiently determined for their demands to be granted. Where would society then end?

Suppose we move to another of the crises of violence with which society has to deal. Communal rioting has broken out; there is burning, killing and looting against a minority sect. Whoever has been near the scene of such events knows the passions that are inflamed and the cruelty with which the mob acts. Families are driven into their houses, surrounded by crowds who scream for their death. Sooner or later the mob climb the fence, throw a can of petrol inside and light it. Here, though, the issue is not as simple as in the customs hall. There has been provocation and counter-provocation; large crowds are involved, carrying by their momentum ordinary passers-by who do not quite know why they are there. The ringleaders are difficult to identify. For the security forces it is a nightmare. Martial law is imposed; there is a curfew, and anyone found breaking it, or looting, is to be shot on sight. But the person breaking the curfew may have been forced out on an errand of mercy. How are the police to fulfil their unenviable duties in accordance with the moral law? Crowds such as these are stopped only if they can see that the security forces mean business.

Sometimes the police are in sympathy with the crowds, and hold back from taking any preventive steps, let alone the extreme measures that are required to end the loss of life. From first-hand evidence I know how terrifying it is and how quickly fear spreads when the victims of a mob know that the police will not protect them. On one such occasion, in a large city that I know well, the Army was called in. The army commander, an outstanding leader, ordered that the first policeman found not carrying out his duty in the face of active rioting was to be shot on sight. Once the police heard this, they quickly changed their minds. I do not think this was an immoral order, nor do I think that the soldier who fired the first shot – if a shot was fired at all; for that I do not know – was acting immorally. What is at stake is not just the lives of those immediately at risk, but the maintenance of law and order, the preservation of society from anarchy. If absolute pacifism were adopted as state policy, the police would be disarmed, and sole possession of firearms yielded to the criminal element of society. What doors this would open to the men of violence, to kidnappers, to those who know how to play on the passions of crowds for their personal ends!

The pacifist will reply that terrorism on the domestic scene cannot be equated with war between nations, and that a different set of principles applies to each. Clearly there is a great difference in the scale of destruction, and no war will ever be as clear-cut with regard to culpability and innocence as in the airport incident. Nevertheless the two are similar in nature: in both, one group is unlawfully using armed force to overpower the other. The pacifist replies that the morally correct response to military invasion is to accept defeat. In this way there will be little, if any, loss of life; the aggressor will ultimately be won over by the good example his victim has set; and even if this were not the case the Christian should be ready to accept whatever suffering life has to offer. This was how Christ overcame his enemies, it is agreed, and it is to this that his followers are called.

For a man to renounce his fundamental right of self-defence when attacked, and to lay down his life rather than harm his attacker, is indeed an act of profound spiritual significance. But it needs no pointing out that to offer my own life, when it is I alone who is being attacked, and to offer another person's life without at least his implicit consent are totally different propositions. My own life is mine to give – provided I have taken the interests of my dependants into account; the life of another is not. Rather, if the other should be under threat and I am in a position to intervene, he has a right to expect my help.

Another form of pacifism proposes non-violent resistance as an alternative to a military defence. It would have preferred that we had offered no armed resistance to Hitler and instead had countered his occupation of Europe with civil disobedience and peaceful refusal to co-operate. In this way, it is claimed, the occupied countries would gradually become ungovernable, the Nazis would begin to soften, and ultimately peace and freedom would be restored. This is to take an extraordinarily unrealistic view of totalitarian regimes such as that of Hitler. By the time he was finally halted, Hitler had liquidated twenty million innocent men, women and children in his concentration camps. These camps were not, as is sometimes suggested, the product of the war but an integral part of the Nazi system designed to deal with people who were regarded as dangerous or racially unacceptable. On top of this his military aggression led to the death of another thirty million or more people.

The proponents of this view concede that for it to work a high degree of preparation and training of the population would be required, equivalent to that given to the armed forces in peacetime. They also agree that the nation would have to be as co-ordinated in its response as in time of war, and fired by as great a dedication. How this could be is difficult to see. The aggressor, moreover, would not hesitate to suppress any organised resistance with all means at his disposal. He would eliminate all leaders, put a prohibition on travel, make effective communication impossible and declare refusal to work illegal. Some he would threaten with imprisonment and violence, whilst others he would entice by the offer of privilege and power; and there are always those willing to collaborate. If food or other essential supplies became short, the population, not the occupying forces and their collaborators, would suffer. Modern technology has enabled the totalitarian state to exercise so great a power of surveillance and intelligence gathering over its citizens that organised resistance becomes virtually impossible; as is abundantly demonstrated in Poland, a nation where only 3 per cent of the population are committed communists and yet whose government, under the direction of the Soviet Union, can hold the rest in check. The more integrated human society becomes, the stronger the grip that a malevolent regime is able to exercise on the nation it has overpowered, and the more important it becomes to block the road to aggression. Pacifism would leave that road unguarded and open to anyone who had his reasons for walking it. Apart from classical antiquity, pacifism of some degree has existed throughout history, but it has always been a minority view, the possession of a small but dedicated group, and has never been tested, let alone adopted as national policy. Some will see in this a sign that nations are lacking in judgement, others that the pacifist proposition lacks a realistic base.

The history of mankind is as much the history of war as it is of peace. There is nothing in recent times to suggest that war, or the threat of it, will not continue to be used to great effect against nations that are militarily inferior. Armed force is one of the ways in which man seeks to further his perceived interests, either as victim or aggressor, at all levels of human society. It originates in the inner, spiritual conflict between Good and Evil, the consequence of the fall, and man cannot hope to be free from its threat until that fundamental conflict is finally resolved. Someone has said that if only there were more and better Christians war would cease, but is this true? It seems rather that of its very nature Evil feels compelled to attack everything that is holy and good; that proportionately as Good predominates, Evil resorts to more extreme measures, the ultimate of which is violence. How else can one explain the relentless fury of the attack against Jesus mounted by the Pharisees and Saduccees, who saw his spiritual teaching as a threat to their own authority? He went about doing good, holding no temporal power, accompanied by only a handful of uninfluential followers. Yet the hostile presence of Satan was ever near him; he was hounded, his every word scrutinised, his actions noted and reported back to the authorities, until finally when no cause could be found against him he was forcefully eliminated. This is not to pass political judgement on any particular nation but only to point to the desperate struggle in which man is engaged, individually and collectively; the Good within each of us trying to gain mastery over Evil; the powers of darkness fighting to retain their unlawful and malign influence on our human family.

Pacifism is quite correct in saying that Evil is not overcome by physical force, but it is mistaken in denying force any rôle at all. Force belongs to the material order and is therefore powerless to destroy Evil in its essence, but Evil operates through the actions of men, and it is at this level that force is able to have a restraining effect by limiting the opportunities Evil has for intimidating and harming the innocent. No one, for instance, would suggest that prisons and policemen are a means of converting the lawbreaker, let alone the hardened criminal, but this is not put forward as a reason for dispensing with their services. What is true on the domestic scene is also true on the international scene.

There remains, however, another face of pacifism, a positive and edifying one. Armed defence can help contain the forces of aggression and violence in the world, but it does not serve the cause of peace in any meaningful sense unless the nation that it seeks to protect is itself committed to peace. Peace is not merely the absence of war; neither can we say that people living under a tyrannical and oppressive regime are living in peace, even if no fighting is taking place. Peace is the consequence, the priceless fruit, of justice. Justice is the gateway that leads to peace, and injustice, itself the first violence, the dangerous slope that leads ultimately to war. If the cause of peace and freedom requires that we close our frontiers to the would-be aggressor, it equally requires that we open our hearts to the claims of the poor, the deprived and those oppressed by injustice wherever they may be. The contribution of pacifism is that it forces us to remember these values, and that it attacks our human tendency to place too much trust in the power of weapons and in purely rational lines of argument.

6. Nuclear Hope

For the pacifist, the advent of nuclear weapons has substantially increased the force and urgency of his case. He can now present the choice facing mankind in simple and clear-cut terms: either destruction of the nation, possibly even extinction of the greater part of mankind, or accepting a Soviet invasion of Europe and making the best one can of the unpleasant consequences. Not unnaturally, he plays down the harm and suffering that such an invasion would inflict, and suggests that the example of turning the other cheek in the true Christian tradition will shame the occupying forces and ultimately convert them into friends and allies. The Christian pacifist points to the fact that Christ redeemed the world through suffering and that he said, 'Whoever will be my disciple must pick up his cross and follow me.' Consequently, he argues, we should see whatever suffering Soviet domination might bring as an opportunity of fulfilling our Christian vocation and overcoming Evil by Good. This reveals the pacifist as a consistent and logical thinker who appeals to high spiritual principles in support of his case. But the proposition 'better red than dead', compelling though it undoubtedly is, conceals a trap; better still is neither the one nor the other, neither nuclear war nor subjection to an alien and hostile regime. The majority of people seem to sense this, for the electorates of the main western nations have clearly indicated that they do not want to be left defenceless.

The problem then arises: how in the nuclear age can one ensure a defence which on the one hand is effective, and on the other morally acceptable? From now onwards we move into unknown and uncharted territory. Nuclear war has never been fought, and we have no sure means of gauging how two adversaries would react if one of them were to fire a nuclear weapon. It is possible to argue that the dynamics of interaction between the opposing forces would compel an ever-increasing level of escalation; it is also possible to argue that the shock of having crossed the nuclear threshold might bring the fighting to an abrupt halt, through the realisation that anything is better than the total destruction of one's homeland. We may hold the most passionate views on this, one way or the other, but we still do not actually know. The one thing we do know, and about which no doubt is admissible, is that all-out strategic nuclear war would spell the end of Europe, the Soviet Union, the United States and much more besides. But the fear and sheer revulsion that this prospect causes could just as well hustle us into reaching the wrong conclusion as lead us to the right one.

This fear that we feel is not new, a consequence only of the nuclear age; it was already being experienced as a major decision-making factor in the years leading up to World War Two. The RAF had been asked to prepare an estimate of the damage to cities that could be expected from aerial bombardment, and, on the evidence of the Spanish Civil War and their own peacetime exercises, came to a conclusion that gave a grossly exaggerated picture. This had a profound effect on government thinking, and particularly on Chamberlain. It is said that as he took off for Munich to meet Hitler, he looked down on the houses of Croydon beneath him and was overwhelmed by the thought of what would happen to them if he failed to reach a compromise with Nazi Germany. But under his starboard wing as he came in to land at Munich lay Dachau, the first of Hitler's concentration camps, whose infamous activities had been amply reported to Whitehall. Here was a far truer pointer to the nature and the scale of the danger that Europe faced; yet there is no indication that Chamberlain gave it even a glance. If kept in proportion, fear of danger is wholesome and to be nourished by all of us, but once it becomes excessive it can cloud one's judgement and even, as in the case of Munich, contribute to the very catastrophe it seeks to avert.

The present nuclear debate concentrates so single-mindedly on the terrible nature of nuclear weapons, that hardly any attention seems to be paid to the nature of conventional war and to what would happen to Europe were this to break out. In many people's minds there is an unspoken assumption that only nuclear weapons threaten Europe's survival, and that if they could once be negotiated away the dread catastrophe we all fear would be averted. There is a further assumption in some minds that if we were to upgrade and strengthen NATO's conventional capability we could dispense with our nuclear weapons and still be adequately defended. These issues are central to the debate, but are not faced up to properly; in short, they are fudged. Both assumptions are dangerously false.

Let us begin by looking at conventional war between the superpowers in order to determine what moral judgement we can make. Conventional war lies within our known and personal experience; we have the data, the historical verdicts and the living testimony of those whom it has affected to enable us to make an informed judgement. We see beyond shadow of doubt the miscalculations that bring such catastrophes about; the unfounded belief each side has at the outset that it will soon all be over; the passion and commitment with which they are fought; the difficulty with which they are brought to an end. 'Far more easily do nations fall into wars', it has been aptly said, 'than ever they fall out of them.' Once the Normandy invasion had succeeded, it was self-evident that the war was lost to Germany, but Hitler would have happily brought everything down with him rather than acknowledge defeat. When finally cornered, he committed suicide with the words, 'They weren't worthy of me.' Like the majority of aggressor-dictators he was a nihilist: either the world bows to him, or the world can go to hell. In Japan, other than their being in no way tainted by Nazi-ism, it was not very different; surrender, the ultimate degradation of the soldier's spirit, did not feature in the military dictionary, and therefore was not an admissible option. Had a way of laying down their arms without the disgrace of military defeat not offered itself, I dare not think what the casualties and material devastation would have been. With the Russians approaching from the West, bent on winning a post-war presence in Tokyo, and the Americans from the South East, their attitudes totally changed by Soviet aggressiveness in Eastern Europe, casualties could have far exceeded MacArthur's estimate of three million.

As to the total casualties in the two world wars, no one will ever know the exact figure. The first war is thought to have cost 25 million, of whom approximately 8 were military and the remainder civilian, who died of disease, starvation and other causes directly attributable to the war. In the second, in Europe alone, at least 50 million were lost, of whom 33 million were civilians. Thus in each war two civilians died for every soldier. These figures may be disputed as to detail but not in their general purport. They tell a story that, for some reason I do not understand, is largely overlooked in the nuclear debate. The truth is that when major wars are fought over densely populated areas such as Europe, huge civilian casualties are an unavoidable consequence of the land fighting. Civilians find themselves caught between the opposing armies, either pinned down by constant shelling, or driven from their homes and unable to decide in which direction to flee for greater safety. They fall victim to disease, malnutrition and despair, and so long as the battle lasts can find no one to organise relief for them.

This is not what the liberating, or defending, armies want; the very reverse. It is just that, other than on the rare occasions when they can afford to declare a city 'open', as with Rome, the nature of modern land-warfare leaves no alternative. In a life-and-death struggle such as we are talking about, only victory will bring an end to the suffering. Could the besieged Soviet army in Leningrad, for instance, have given those unable to influence the course of the fighting, such as the old and the very young, the same rations and care as the front-line troops? In that one terrible battle in excess of 600,000 civilians died, half as many again as in the entire bomber offensive against Germany.

What has gone wrong with the conduct of the defence debate is that the destructive horror of nuclear weapons has taken our attention away from the other horror of an East-West conventional war. The two are not, of course, of the same magnitude; but that is not the point. What we need to ask ourselves is whether all-out conventional war in Europe is a morally acceptable eventuality, and this the great majority of us have failed to do. Or if we have, then we are showing remarkably little moral sensitivity.

Given that twice as many died in the first as in the second war, we must reckon with the possibility that a third conventional war would follow approximately the same progression. That means casualties in tens of millions, very possibly many tens of millions, and a devastated Europe. One may argue that war in Europe does not necessarily mean all-out war, that it would more probably be fought for a limited objective, which the aggressor had judged he could quickly win without risk of escalation. But it is exactly in this kind of way that so many major wars have started in the past, the aggressor misjudging his victim's reaction and setting in motion an ever-escalating train of consequences that he never foresaw. Hitler gambled on a policy of a quick pounce, hold tight and wait; then, after an interval, another pounce, in the belief that the other side would accept the *fait accompli* rather than risk a full-scale counter attack. First it was the Rhineland, then Austria, then Czechoslovakia. But the next pounce brought all-out war to Europe. The Japanese military ruling clique made a similar kind of miscalculation. Their foe was really Britain, not America; they wanted to throw the alien Western intruder out of Asia and return Asia to the Asians with herself as their leader. The one obstacle in their way was the American fleet, and this they had to neutralise. If it were eliminated in one sudden attack, whilst peacefully sleeping at Pearl Harbor, the 'effete' Americans would never embark upon the prodigious task of reconquering the vast regions of the distant Pacific. What a fateful misjudgement!

This is the first thing that needs to be said about conventional war, and which we must not try to sidestep. If nuclear weapons are assumed not to exist, conventional war may still appear what aggressors have so often thought it to be, a rational option of state policy. There is no contemporary evidence to encourage the belief that never again will major nations succumb to the temptation to use conventional weapons against each other, where they have the incentive and are led to think that they will get away with it.

What are we to conclude from this? So far the debate has revolved round the different aspects of nuclear war and has said very little about the rights and wrongs of conventional war. The popular cry has been, 'We want to be defended, but not with nuclear weapons', and the general thinking that once rid of nuclear weapons we shall all be able to breathe freely once again, East as well as West. But is this true? I do not think so at all. I think we would find that we were in greater danger by far than we are at present. I think that too many of us are looking only at one part of the problem and not at the problem as a whole. In any case, when one considers what another war in Europe would mean, I find it a dubious morality that aims to abolish the nuclear deterrent only to replace it with an upgraded conventional defence. It implies, or at least risks implying, that all-out conventional war in defence of Europe is morally tolerable, and this I cannot accept. There are three potential disasters that confront us: nuclear war, conventional war, and subjugation by an alien regime. The three cannot be equated in terms of horror, but they are all none the less disastrous. The only solution I can accept as adequately satisfying the moral imperative is the one which prevents all of them. This is what the deterrent claims to do, not only for us in the West, but for the Warsaw Pact nations too.

What is new is not just the immense destructive power of nuclear weapons, and the long-lasting genetic and ecological effect of radiation, but the simultaneous development of the long-range rocket. For the first time it is possible for one state to cripple another far removed from its borders without having to assemble and despatch an invasion force. In this way nuclear weapons have totally changed the nature of war. They have changed it because, if invoked, they trump every other weapon. With the use of battlefield nuclear weapons you can hold the enemy attack on the battlefield; in some people's view you can replace your battlefield nuclear weapons with an upgraded and more sophisticated conventional capability and still perhaps hold him; but if your adversary then invokes his strategic weapons and threatens the destruction of your homeland, the battlefield victory has served no purpose. It is not at that level that the war will ultimately be lost or won. You can do the same to your attacker, of course, and threaten his homeland too with your own strategic weapons. If he should pre-empt you by an unannounced first strike, no matter how massive, you still have the power to hit back equally hard. What, one may well ask, was the point of the conventional war in the first place? You fight to the limit of your resources; the land over which the battle raged is devastated; hundreds of thousands of lives are sacrificed, perhaps even tens of millions; and in terms of final outcome you end up where you began, with the battle of wills over the nuclear strategic strike. If, God forbid, this is invoked, the two sides have embarked upon a venture that will destroy both of them.

This is the second thing that needs to be said about conventional war. It is the gateway, almost certainly the only gateway, to nuclear war, for hardly anybody seriously thinks that war would start with an all-out pre-emptive strike. It would be a win-all or lose-all gamble on one throw of the dice, with the odds heavily stacked against success.

The implication of this is clear and unarguable. To renounce unilaterally one's whole nuclear capability is to leave oneself with no effective defence against an adversary who has retained his own capability and who, if the prize were sufficiently important to him and the political repercussions bearable, might be tempted to use it, or at least threaten to use it. This would leave the nuclear side in a position of total and irreversible military superiority with no counterbalancing force on the international political scene, and thus create a situation unprecedented in the history of man. The nuclear power would know that he could never be threatened by the other's conventional forces, no matter how formidable they might be. He would merely have to declare that he was not prepared to accept military action as an acceptable way of resolving disputes between superpowers, and that if attacked he would invoke some form of nuclear strike against the other's territory.

One may think that he would not dare to do this because of the international opprobrium it would attract. But he could quite easily construct a strong propaganda case in his own favour, along the lines that war between major powers was the scourge of mankind and no longer tolerable; that one sharp lesson was the way of putting an end to it once and for all; and that the offending power was only getting what he deserved. After all, he might not need to fire his weapons, merely threaten to do so, for the other side could never afford to call his bluff, if bluff it were.

Other major consequences follow. Having renounced one's nuclear weapons, would there be any point in maintaining the huge conventional capability hitherto required for defence against a full-scale conventional attack? If an attack should come, what moral or military justification could there be for a fight to the death to repulse it, when the adversary can demand surrender at any moment under threat of a nuclear strike? Since he holds the trump card, why would he incur the expense and risk of an all-out conventional attack? Aggressors have acquired great expertise in contriving incidents of one kind or another which make it look as if they are the victims of aggression.

If there were something he really wanted, it would not be difficult so to manoeuvre as to force the other to surrender, and still claim to be acting within his rights.

One is entitled to argue that the Soviet Union of today would never act in such a way, were the West to renounce unilaterally its nuclear weapons. But, even if such a judgement were sound, one cannot argue that no future Soviet government, let alone other possible totalitarian regimes for the rest of time, ever would so act. For fifty years Marxism-Leninism consistently preached that a final military showdown would be needed to finish off capitalism. Stalin said to Tito in 1956 that the sole reason France was not communist was that the Soviet Army had not entered Paris. Only when it was realised that nuclear war would almost certainly destroy communism as well as capitalism was the doctrine of the inevitability of war rejected, and detente substituted.

To say that the Soviet Union might one day use force against the West if she thought that to do so would assist the cause of communism is in no way to be derogatory. The Marxist-Leninist sees world peace as coming about only when communism has spread to the entire international community; he genuinely believes that in spreading the world revolution he is serving the good of humanity. The Soviet Union repudiates Christian morality, and holds that the good of communism is the primary criterion of what is moral and what is not; it has never sought to conceal its belief that if armed force can serve the communist cause, then it is right to use it. That from the time of Krushchev on it has seen the nuclear deterrent as an absolute barrier to the use of force against the West is a matter of great significance. From a different standpoint than ours it confirms that nuclear weapons have totally changed the nature of war; it means that, deeply divided though the Soviet Union and the Western Alliance are in so many ways, they are wholly united in the knowledge that nuclear war would destroy both of them. This in turn means that initiating conventional war, which prior to the nuclear age had always been seen as a rational option of state policy, now ceases so to be, since neither of the superpowers can be sure that it will not escalate to all-out nuclear war. The sheer destructiveness of the weapon and the elusiveness and range of the delivery system makes nuclear war unwinnable, and therefore not a road that anyone in their senses can take.

One cannot, unfortunately, say that a nuclear attack by one side against the other is absolutely impossible, only that it is rationally impossible. For this reason, and because of the moral problems that nuclear deterrence involves, many people see the ultimate and only fully satisfactory solution as lying in the total abolition of all nuclear weapons. But let us suppose that the seemingly impossible has happened. All existing nuclear nations have destroyed their weapons, dismantled their manufacturing plants and solemnly undertaken never to build another weapon, never to engage in weaponry research, and never to communicate nuclear technology to another nation. Where would this leave us?

Firstly, the use of armed force once more becomes a rational option for the superpowers and this brings back the grim spectre of world war. One may say, 'Yes, but this time we have learnt our lesson. A way will be found, simply because it must be found.' I do not believe it. The spirit of violence in the world is growing, not diminishing. Nations, and their allies, have to be their own policemen, and who can police a superpower other than another superpower? If one of them thinks he can gain some advantage through the use of force and get away with it, can we really say that the temptation will never prove too great, even for the best of leaders, let alone the worst? We cannot be sure that the world will never see another Hitler. If nuclear war is thought to be a real possibility, even though manifestly suicidal, it is hardly rational to argue that, the deterrent once removed, conventional war is highly unlikely. Should such a war break out, each superpower would almost certainly set about regaining a nuclear capability, convinced that the other was doing the same, and with the carefully worked-out balances of the era of deterrence no longer there, a most dangerous and volatile crisis would confront mankind.

Secondly, nuclear knowledge cannot be disinvented; it will remain with us to the end of time, to be put to the service of mankind in more ways than we can at present foresee. The ever-accelerating advance of technology will make manufacture of all forms of nuclear power simpler and cheaper, and will ultimately bring weaponry within reach of any nation or major political grouping that has a strong enough incentive to acquire it. Can we be sure that no other nation would fall to the temptation? Extremism is another feature of today's world, among regimes and individual national leaders as well as at lower levels of society; possession of the decisive weapon could one day appear to one of these as the means of fulfilling what they see to be their God-given mission. Then where would we be? As things stand today, the superpowers might well join forces to stop him, for the last thing either of them wants is nuclear war triggered off by an irresponsible third party. But should they cease to be nuclear, the position radically alters. With the restraint of the deterrent gone, and armed force once more a potential factor in superpower rivalry, one can picture all kinds of dangers. If smaller powers started to become nuclear, the major ones would almost certainly feel they had to follow suit for their own safety, and the last state might well be worse than the first.

Pondering this vexed question, and reading and listening to the widely differing viewpoints that are put forward, evokes the memory of that fearsome atomic column, engulfing Nagasaki at its base and higher at its peak than any man-made object had ever before reached. To have to live with the horror which that single bomb caused is a harrowing experience and a source of great personal regret; but I find that the very fact of thinking about it immediately recalls the infinitely greater horror that the totality of the war up until that moment had constituted 55,000,000 killed and nobody knows how many maimed in one way or another for the rest of their lives. Then there is the further thought of the other millions who would have had to die, had the bomb not cut the war short. To reply that it might not have come to all-out war across the length and breadth of Japan is no adequate reply at all. Japan's surrender did not hinge round the wording of the Potsdam Declaration, nor upon the prospect of imminent and inevitable military defeat. To the military who governed, honour was more important than the survival of the nation, and honour could be preserved only by death to the last. 'A hundred million may die,' they argued, 'but the national spirit will live on.'

The atom bombs over Hiroshima and Nagasaki did not inflict as many casualties as the heaviest conventional attacks, either in Germany or Japan, but they proved decisive; they achieved in just twelve days what the bomber offensive kept hoping it could achieve but never quite could. The full implication of the bomb's power to end a world war is obscured by the fact that it was available only at a time when the Allies were already closing in on Japan. We have not stopped to ask what would have been the result had it been ready earlier.

The race to build the bomb had been against Germany, not Japan. The Commando and SOE raids on the heavy water plant in Norway in 1942/3 indicate the seriousness with which the Allies viewed this threat, but Hitler saw other secret weapons as more promising, and never gave this his backing. Had he done so, it is just conceivable that he might have snatched victory out of the jaws of defeat. Had the American bomb been ready two years earlier, it would have been used to stop the European war; and in that event half the casualties of World War Two would have been spared; the Western Allies would probably have prevented the division of Europe; there would have been no need for Hiroshima and Nagasaki. What a different post-war world!

'Against me you cannot fight,' the atomic cloud over Nagasaki seemed to me to be calling out to those who witnesssed it. Today it sends out the same call, only more powerfully and more insistently – for what was then only an infant is now a fully grown man – indeed a whole generation of grown men. It is a plain reality, demonstrated by what happened in Japan, that one cannot fight an adversary who has a monopoly of nuclear weapons and the will to use them. Until something new comes along, either in technology or in the structure of international society, which will once again alter the very nature of war, there is no total defence of the nation with conventional weapons only. It follows that our only choice is a straight one between retaining a credible nuclear deterrent, or leaving ourselves with no effective defence at all against the Soviet Union. It is the fact that there is no middle ground between these two poles, no means of abolishing nuclear weapons without also abolishing the right of self-defence against another nuclear power, that creates the moral dilemma, and which accounts for the spiritual and moral agonising that has gone on, particularly within the Christian Church. This is not to say that there never will be middle ground, only that none exists at present.

Not all Christian bodies uphold the right of self-defence if this involves the possession of nuclear weapons, and for these the attempted solution is easier to find. Even so, the harmful consequences of having no adequate defence are to some extent conceded, and efforts made to suggest that alternative forms of defence, not involving the use of nuclear arms, do exist. But there is no agreed consensus as to what the alternative defence should be; there is no full facing up to the obvious fact that against a determined enough nuclear aggressor a conventional-only defence cannot prevail; and there is a tendency to look upon atheistic communism and Western capitalism as equally bad morally. Even so, alternative defence studies have their own contribution to make in building confidence and political stability among nations. It is all too easy to look solely for the ultimate solution and to ignore the small steps that pave the way towards it.

Perhaps more than any other, it is the Catholic Church that demonstrates the agonising of men of goodwill the world over in search of some middle ground. Successive Popes, and the bishops' conferences of major Western nations, have expressed their abhorrence of the use of nuclear weapons and specifically condemned it in relation to indiscriminate attack on populated areas; yet at the same time they have consistently upheld the right of effective self-defence. Since these two themes are hard to reconcile, all statements have had to settle for some form of conditional conclusion. The majority view seems to be that nuclear deterrence is acceptable so long as there is a genuine commitment to arms reduction. Certainly this is what Pope John Paul II said in his address written for the United Nations Special Session on Disarmament, on 11 June 1982:

> In current conditions deterrence based on balance, certainly not as an end in itself but as a stage on the way towards a progressive disarmament, can still be judged morally acceptable. None the less, in order to preserve peace, it is indispensable not to be satisfied with this minimum, which is always susceptible to the real danger of explosion.

Carefully prepared for a world audience, and intended as an expression of his views on defence in the nuclear age, this statement is still open to varying interpretations. It confirms that deterrence as a concept is morally acceptable, but refrains from judging the deterrent as we see it deployed today. It stresses the need to work for a better solution than the present one, with less dependence on weapons, particularly nuclear weapons, but it does not endorse unilateral disarmament. The reference to progressive disarmament reflects the ardent hope of most men's hearts, but it offers little real hope of any substantial change until the present ideological confrontation diminishes.

In a profoundly spiritual study of the great moral issues surrounding the deterrent, the United States bishops go further still, and condemn even the threat to use nuclear weapons for the purposes of deterrence. Yet they conclude that the deterrent may properly be retained, on condition that an undertaking is given that it will never under any circumstances be used. If you ask, how, if the Soviet Union knows it will never be used, can it then deter, and therefore what point is there in having it at all, the answer is given that the Soviet Union cannot be absolutely sure that you would never use it, and that this element of doubt may be just sufficient to deter. As an acceptable political stance this is very difficult to see. You announce solemnly that you will never use your weapons, but you hope that you will not be believed. You employ people to design and build huge engines of destruction, and others to train daily in how to operate them, and all the time it is nothing but make-believe. I cannot picture where it leaves the Soviet Union, nor can I picture how those in the nuclear chain of command would manage to maintain their morale, or even self-respect. I may very well be wrong, but it seems to me a little like asking people to live a lie.

All the same, I think the American bishops' paper is highly significant. Firstly it indicates the lengths to which they feel driven in order to hold the highest possible moral position. Secondly it testifies to their recognition, despite all the moral reservations, that the deterrent does have the capacity to deter, for if they hold that it may deter even under the extreme conditions they impose, how much more so without those conditions? For me, this puts the nuclear dilemma in its true perspective. On the one hand the right of self-defence, which no one but the absolute pacifist denies, leaves no alternative but to retain some credible and effective form of deterrence. On the other, the law that God has implanted in creation, in order that man may live in harmony and attain to his eternal destiny, requires that we do everything in our power to achieve the maximum possible, mutually agreed, and mutually verifiable, arms reduction.

However there are some who argue that deploying the

deterrent involves a daily intention to cause huge civilian casualties should the nation be attacked, and that such an intention makes deterrence a morally unacceptable option. That is to say, no matter how high the probability of the deterrent keeping the peace, nor how disastrous the probable consequences of dismantling it, dismantle we must, on the grounds that an immoral means cannot be used to achieve a good end. It is a moral view that has a number of adherents but I do not believe that it stands.

As a start to examining it we need to remember that what we are facing is an intractable moral dilemma, to which no solution can be found which is wholly free of moral problems. For the Western Alliance to repudiate the possession of nuclear weapons would be to leave their development and deployment for the rest of time to those nations who see no moral objection to using them for their own ends. To advocate this may appear to have solved one moral problem, but only to replace it with another of the direst consequence for the future of mankind.

In order to assess the morality of intention of the soldier who deploys the deterrent, we need to know two things: under what circumstances might he be called upon to press the button; and what would his purpose be in doing so?

The circumstances under which one of the superpowers could take the gigantic risk of launching a major attack on the other are difficult in the extreme to envisage. Since both sides have the power to destroy the other, it could only happen if the aggressor had convinced himself that his victim was not prepared to use nuclear weapons. In the present state of the deterrent, with both East and West making their intentions on this point abundantly clear, such a judgement is virtually inconceivable. The possibility is theoretically there, but in real-life terms hardly at all.

NATO would resort to nuclear use only if an all-out attack were launched on Europe. In such an event her sole aim would be to restore the deterrent; that is to say, to convince the Soviets that they had miscalculated NATO's intentions, and to persuade them to call off the attack. We are here on unknown and unfamiliar ground; we can make our own personal guess as to how the Soviet Union would respond if confronted with the reality that NATO was prepared to retaliate rather than surrender, but we do not actually know what would happen. In any case we are talking in a political and military vacuum; we cannot even imagine the sort of tensions and attitudes that would have had to have built up for such a miscalculation to have been made. Yet the Soviet government is rational and cautious, even if perhaps opportunist. It is not imaginable that she would of her own deliberate choice persist in a course of action that she knew could only end in her own destruction. Similarly the very last thing we in NATO want is our own destruction. Those who deploy the deterrent know that if ever nuclear weapons have to be invoked, they must be used in such a way as to create the most favourable possible conditions for the aggressor to come to his senses. The guiding principle is to use as much as is thought necessary to convince him, but not a fraction more. It stands to reason that if you hit him so hard that he has nothing much more to lose, you will both go under together. One can rightly argue that in time of war passions are aroused and judgements warped, but one can also argue, and with even more force, that once nuclear weapons begin to be used, the two Alliances have absolute mutuality of interest in not pursuing the war a minute longer.

Thus to assert that those in the nuclear chain of command have a daily intention to kill large numbers of civilians is to present a distorted picture of the reality. Only if a major assault were launched against Europe would the possibility of using nuclear weapons come into question, and in that case the intention would be to bring the fighting to an end in the shortest possible time and with the minimum loss of life, not to embark upon the hopeless and suicidal attempt to defeat the attacker by devastating his homeland.

If one holds that to use even the smallest nuclear weapon,

directed against opposing troops, is morally wrong in an absolute sense, then there are grounds for seeing the conditional intention of all those who deploy them as also morally wrong. But in this case it is difficult to see why the same verdict is not passed on those in the conventional chain of command. They are daily preparing for the possibility of all-out war on European soil and anyone who has given the matter even a moment's thought knows that such a war, unless halted early on, would also cause huge civilian casualties, possibly in tens of millions.

That the intention of those who deploy the deterrent is morally wrong is not the view of the great majority of moralists, nor is it the view of the Pope, the bishops' conferences and many other Christian bodies of the Western nations who, with varying qualifications, have held the deterrent to be morally tolerable. Even the American bishops' letter has left a measure of ambiguity as to whether their condemnation of nuclear uses is intended as total, or whether they are prepared to accept the use of some weapons. If there is not an absolute moral imperative forbidding the use of all nuclear weapons at any level and under every conceivable circumstance, then the intention of those who daily deploy them cannot either be absolutely wrong. There may be room for rethinking the manner in which the deterrent is deployed, or adding new safeguards, or something of the sort, but one cannot condemn all forms of nuclear deterrence purely on grounds of the personal intention of those in the nuclear chain of command.

On the other hand, there is world-wide agreement that all-out strategic nuclear use is morally unacceptable. The question on which we cannot agree is, where, along the spectrum that links limited low-yield use to full-scale war, does what is morally tolerable become morally intolerable? I do not see that this can be satisfactorily answered in the abstract, even by a formula such as 'the indiscriminate killing of civilians', for too much depends upon what is at stake and what the use of the nuclear weapons in question can be expected to achieve. The atomic attacks on Hiroshima and Nagasaki, although directed against major military targets, killed many thousands of civilians indiscriminately; yet, because of the fact that they brought the war to an immediate end, thereby saving several millions of lives, there is a compelling case for holding them to be morally tolerable. Can one, then, really say that, in the highly improbable event of an all-out attack on Europe, to threaten a limited nuclear strike on a military but populated target for the clear purpose of halting the aggression, and to have the intention of carrying it out unless the attack is called off, is morally unacceptable? I do not think so. Only because this very intention was in doubt did war break out. To take the one step capable of correcting the error and halting the war cannot be immoral in an absolute sense.

We have come back to the same kind of moral problem that faced us in the airport customs hall, if we just substitute the catastrophe of world war for the gunmen and the deterrent for the armed policeman. The analogy does not entirely fit, if only because the deterrent is holding war at bay and thus preventing the killing from ever having started. To be more exact, we would have to postulate that, so long as the policeman keeps his gun levelled at the gunmen, they themselves dare not shoot. Even so, the analogy is close enough for our purposes.

In the case of the airport hall, the moralists all agree that if the probability of not hitting the boy is high, the policeman is acting properly in shooting. There are also many who hold that even if it is the other way round, he still has a duty to fire, just as one may sometimes be forced to sacrifice the life of an innocent hostage rather than give in to an impossible demand, for the reason that to do so will make kidnapping an easy option.

Although the horror of a nuclear exchange cannot, in any way, be compared with massacring the occupants of a customs hall, it is not clear why the moral verdict as to intention should be different. In the case of the deterrent, only a conditional intention at most exists; the deterrent has always so far deterred, and there is a high probability that it will continue to do so. Both sides prepare daily to use it, of course; but neither of them anticipates actually having to do so, for they are convinced that by deploying it they are preserving a mutual and assured peace.

The pacifist position I fully understand. I do not agree with it, but I find it consistent as to war, even if not so consistent when it comes to the domestic scene. The in-between position, which upholds the right of self-defence but denies the weapons with which to exercise it, I do not understand, though I respect it. I know that in defence matters, particularly, we have to strive to our utmost to identify and then hold the high moral ground. I know that we are fallible, our personal motives suspect, even the best of us, and our reasoning is by no means as dependable as we like to think. I know that we are pulled in many direc-tions, subject to many dubious influences, and that we have to open ourselves to the possibility that the invisible and incomprehensible God may want us to follow a course that to human reason seems sheer madness. If it were clear that He wanted us to give up nuclear arms and accept the consequences, we would have to do so; He can want nothing that is contrary to our real good and, if we lose everything else, we must at all costs not lose faith in this.

If God were asking us to dismantle the deterrent, how could we tell? Certainly not through a process of reasoning alone. Nor would the testimony of individuals suffice, even if they claimed a divine revelation; for according to Christian belief, God completed his full and final revelation to man when he sent us His Son, Jesus Christ.

> In many and various ways God spoke of old to our fathers by the prophets: but in these last days he has spoken to us by a Son, whom he appointed heir of all things and through whom also he created the world. [Heb. 1:1,2.]

Although God continues to speak after His mysterious fashion to each individual human heart, it is now through the Church that He speaks to mankind as a whole. Individuals play their part in prompting the Church, and those who hold strong views on an important moral issue which they feel is authenticated by some interior revelation or by cogent argument may well carry many Christians with them. But such a message would not have validity for the whole of Christianity unless the Church were to declare unequivocally that it is a precept binding on all its members. In respect of unilateral nuclear disarmament, this has clearly not happened.

Some people seem to think it a small thing that we have come forty years without war in Europe, and draw little comfort for the future from it. Instead they feel the need, in the interests of peace, to keep our attention focused on the potential threat of nuclear weapons, and to persuade us that there is an ever-increasing danger of nuclear war breaking out. That is not the way my personal experience since those dark days of World War Two moves me to see it. I believe that the most dangerous nuclear phase was the opening one, and that were there going to be war between the superpowers, it would have come then, during the time that both were testing each other out and before the stark reality of the deterrent had fully struck home. Superpowers give a high priority to retaining their international status, and their respective governments give an equal priority to staying in office. No doubt they would be happy to see their own international influence stronger and their rival's diminished; no doubt, too they will go to extreme lengths to further their own perceived interest. But that they should knowingly and intentionally put their very survival at risk is hardly credible.

Whatever their differences, whatever the means either may adopt in order to gain an advantage over the other, in this one matter of survival their mutual interests are indissolubly linked. The last thing they want is nuclear war by accident or nuclear war imposed on them by a third party, whether ally or adversary. We can be assured that their mutuality of interest in this respect will drive them to take every possible precaution, now greatly helped by advancing technology, to ensure that neither of these two things happen.

In any case, war of the magnitude that we are talking about, even if aimed at a limited objective, can come about only as a result of a major and collective decision-making process. There has to be some compelling motivation, a virtual certainty of succeeding without suffering a retaliatory strike, and a co-ordinated, and therefore detectable, military build-up. It cannot suddenly happen as a result of a handful of senior officers, or even the president himself, suddenly taking leave of their senses.

These past forty years seem to me to mark a decisive stage in human history, in that they have banished from our beautiful earth the terrible spectre of world war. From now onwards whoever wishes to walk the road towards world conquest, which throughout the whole of recorded history has so attracted men of power, some of them evil, some merely self-seeking, will find their way blocked by that deadly cloud which, in its infancy, stood as a sentinel over Hiroshima and Nagasaki. If ever that cloud is entered, there is no possibility of emerging alive.

I believe that the wilderness through which we have marched since 1945, disappointed that victory never brought us the kind of peace we thought it would, and disunited because of uncertainty as to which road to take in such a rapidly changing world, is behind us, and that different territory altogether lies ahead. I believe that as we become more familiar with nuclear power, we will feel less fearful of it, more aware that if we behave responsibly we can hold it under proper control, and more conscious of the many ways in which it can be harnessed for our common good. The very fact that nuclear nations can no longer afford to fight each other, and that world war has been relegated to what Pope John Paul movingly called 'the tragic past', is already a momentous step forward. True, we are not protected from smaller wars, nor from the perhaps greater danger of globally organised terrorism or subversion, but there is hope that the continuing advance of weapons technology over the whole spectrum will gradually compel the world community to find ways of muzzling the freedom of nations to fight each other.

There is, I believe, a lesson to be learnt from the experience of the Jews during their forty-year journey across the desert to the promised land. They knew that God had chosen them from among the nations for a unique rôle in the fulfilment of His hidden plan, and that so long as they obeyed His voice He would watch over them and guide their steps. Of this they had tangible and undeniable proof, and in Moses they had one of the great leaders of all time; yet they kept rebelling, insisting on their own way and as a result losing their sense of direction. What saved them was a succession of threats to their common survival, and ultimately the powerful and moving prayer of Moses. We, too, are journeying into the unknown. The nuclear age is giving us power to reshape the world to a degree that former generations would never have conceived possible. Vast horizons of opportunity are opening up before us, in the sort of way it must have appeared to the Jews when they reached Mount Nebo, on the frontiers of the Promised Land which was to become their home. At that stage they felt their inadequacy, they knew that they could succeed only if God helped and guided them. Do we realise this? Or are we so absorbed in our new technology, and so carried away by our newly acquired power over the created world, power even to reshape human embryos, that we see no need for any guide other than our own reasoning processes? If what we have in mind is to reshape the world just according to our own ideas, it has no hope of becoming that unique and unimaginable masterpiece that God in His wisdom and insight has destined it to be. Instead we will be heading only for disaster.

We may be sure that Satan is doing his best to divert us from this urgent task, by sowing discord, agitating our minds, persuading us that now at last we can become masters of our own destiny. The one thing he does not want us to see is that it is from the heart, not the weapon, that come wars and enmities – indeed all the ills that beset human existence; just as from here come all the good and the greatness of which man is capable. Whatever needs to be done at the international level in restoring confidence between opposing blocs, removing poverty and oppression, helping the developing countries to become economically stronger, it is at the very deepest level of all, in our inmost hearts, that the struggle for peace has to begin. Peace requires an inner conversion of heart, continually renewed; it requires us to live our lives in a spirit of unselfishness and openness to others, so to transform our hearts and our sense of priorities that in all our decisions we take into account the good of the whole of mankind as well as our own good. Where we in the West are particularly at fault is that we leave no stone unturned in securing the defences of our own freedom, but give a low priority to confronting the extremes of poverty and injustice that oppress so great a part of the human family, and which after their own manner are also enemies and destroyers of freedom.

For us as individuals the question that most needs answering is: what can we ourselves do to help build a safer and more liveable world, one that better conforms to the dignity of man? At the end of the war, in my own small way, I was asking a similar question, but without finding an answer. Part of my problem was that I felt that whatever I undertook had to be big enough to make a real impact. I wanted to be up and doing, engaged upon something important, and not losing time. Well, we have to commit ourselves heart and soul to action, sometimes to action of great public importance, but if we are all the time doing and speaking, our words will end by being just words, and our actions just actions. These actions and these words need power in order to carry our their intended purpose, and this requires that we carve out time to be still and to cultivate the habit of prayer. There is an old monastic maxim: 'If prayer is right, everything is right. For prayer will not let anything go wrong.' Prayer revitalises and gives meaning to everything we do; it is through prayer that we are led step by step along the path of God's hidden plan. In our busy and noisy world, prayer is the missing factor.

The prayer I am thinking of is not so much the prayer of asking, as the prayer of silence. It is an entering into the inner room of our heart and closing the door, just to be alone with God who dwells there and wants to communicate Himself. When He communicates it is in a form that is always a sending, always a call to journey forth from the security and self-enclosure of our private world and hopes, in order to fulfil some mission, to achieve some good purpose. To Abraham he said, 'Go forth from your country and your kindred and your father's house to the land I shall show you. And I will make of you a great nation.' (Gen. 12:1.) To Moses, 'Come, and I will send you to Pharoah that you may bring forth my people, the sons of Israel, out of Egypt.' (Exod. 3:10.) To the frightened and bewildered disciples sitting behind locked doors, the risen Christ appeared and said: 'Peace be with you', and immediately followed it with the words, 'As the Father has sent me, even so I send you.' (John 20:21.) These are the great calls that stand out as turning points of history, and calls such as these do not come very often. But to all of us in one form or another, either interiorly or through the circumstances of our daily lives, God is ever calling, wanting us to understand the depth and the reality of His love. 'Behold I have graven you on the palms of my hand . . . . You are precious in my eyes, and honoured, and I love you.' (Isaiah 49:16; 43:4.) He calls in order that His self-giving love may fill our hearts, and give power and direction and warmth to our words and our actions, so that we in turn can communicate that love to others.

If this is the God who, while dwelling in our hearts, has called us forward into the nuclear age, I do not see that we have to fear, so long as we listen to His voice.

Selected Bibliography

Butow, Robert J.C., *Japan's Decision to Surrender* (Stanford University, USA, 1954).

Chinnock, Frank, *Nagasaki – The Forgotten Bomb* (George Allen and Unwin, London, 1970).

Falls, Cyril, *The First World War* (Longmans, London, 1960).

Groves, Leslie, *Now It Can Be Told* (André Deutsch, London, 1963).

Johnson, Mgr Vernon, *One Lord, One Faith,* (Sheed and Ward, London, 1945).

Laurence, William L., *Dawn Over Zero,* (Knopf, New York, 1946).

——, 'The Story of the Atomic Bomb' (*The New York Times,* 1946).

Morton, Louis, *The Decision to Use the Atomic Bomb,* Command Decisions (Harcourt Bruce, New York).

Thomas, Gordon and Morgan Witts, Max, *Ruin from the Air* (Hamish Hamilton, London, 1977).

Toland, John, *The Rising Sun* (Bantam Books, New York, 1970).

van der Post, Laurens, *The Night of the New Moon* (The Hogarth Press, London, 1970).

The author is grateful to the following for permission to reproduce quoted material:

Laurens van der Post and The Hogarth Press (*The Night of the New Moon*); Curtis Brown and William Laurence (*Dawn Over Zero*). The extract from *The First World War* is reprinted by kind permission of Curtis Brown on behalf of the estate of Cyril Falls; first published 1960 by Longmans.

Index